KT-368-557

THE NOVELS OF
CHARLES KINGSLEY

A Christian Social Interpretation

ALLAN JOHN HARTLEY

THE HOUR-GLASS PRESS
FOLKESTONE

EDINBURGH UNIVERSITY LIBRARY

CANCELLED

Published in Great Britain by the Hour-Glass Press,
Bailey Brothers and Swinfen Ltd.

ISBN 0 561 01000 5

Copyright © 1977 by Allan John Hartley

All rights reserved, including the right to reproduce this book,
or portions thereof, in any form, except for the inclusion of
brief quotations in a review

Printed in Great Britain at the Alden Press, Oxford

CHARLES KINGSLEY, 1860

Reproduced from a copy of the engraving by Lowes Dickinson

Courtesy of Captain L. C. E. Ayre CBE RN

Contents

Preface

Charles Kingsley's contribution to the Christian Social Movement was his parcel of novels, and this treatise is intended to clarify his deeper purposes in them, while the detailed analyses of their respective themes and structural plots are aimed at spelling out the spiritual solution of this high-minded and patriotic clergyman for curing the ills of his society.

Kingsley was stimulated by Carlyle's approach to the 'condition of England', but he owed his deepest debt to Frederick Denison Maurice, from whom he acquired a view of Christianity that, like Augustine's, 'explained all heaven and earth'. From Maurice emanated an intellectual influence that inspired and informed Kingsley's own, and it is the contention of the present writer that Kingsley's novels can only be fully appreciated in terms of his Coleridgean mentor. But Maurice was difficult, less for what he said than for the maieutic way in which he said it; and while his style veiled him from many, it nevertheless gave his work a spiritual and poetic tone that fascinated literary men like Tennyson, Thomas Hughes, and Kingsley – all of whom were driven to translate his philosophical abstractions for the common reader. So adept was Kingsley in this regard that his novels not infrequently suggest juvenilia. In fact, however, they are imaginative and popular interpretations of the great theologian's ideas, and it is time that we read them for their Christian message as dramatized by Kingsley for the redemption of society.

The Water Babies is not included in this study, not because it is not imbued with the same high moral purposes as the novels, but because as a children's fantasy including observations on natural phenomena, it lies outside the general plan of this work. But in it as in his other fiction, Kingsley wrapped his parable in 'seeming Tom-fooleries', not only to show the doubting Thomases of the world that there is 'a miraculous and divine element underlying all physical nature', but more importantly, to convince them that they know nothing about anything 'in the sense in which they may know God in Christ, and right and wrong'.

Dalhousie University: January 1976   A.J.H.

Acknowledgments

I remember with gratitude the kindness of the late Miss G. Lilian M. Vallings, the adopted daughter of Lucas Malet (Charles Kingsley's daughter), who, as Kingsley's literary executrix, allowed me to copy unpublished letters still in copyright; and I am equally grateful to her niece, Mrs. Angela Covey-Crump, for allowing me to use them in the present study.

Copies of other unpublished letters pertaining to the novels and used in this text were obtained through the kind permission of the officials in the following institutions: the British Library; the University Library, Cambridge; the Morris L. Parrish Collection of Victorian Novelists, Princeton; the Pierpont Morgan Library, New York; and the Rare Book Room in the Library of the University of Illinois at Urbana-Champaign.

I am also grateful to Geoffrey Bullough, Emeritus Professor, University of London, under whose direction I was researching when the extent of Kingsley's debt to Maurice first became apparent; and I am especially indebted to Dr. J. M. S. Tompkins, who not only encouraged the pursuit of Kingsley, but gave me the benefit of her kindly and constructive criticism.

By permission of the editors of *Theology*, Mr. R. J. Brookes and the Rev. Professor G. R. Dunstan, I have drawn on my article in the December, 1967, issue of that periodical.

And, lastly, I record my thanks to the Canada Council for two summer grants and a Leave Fellowship; and to the administration of Dalhousie University for a leave of absence (1971–2).

... Charles Kingsley spoke during two hours and twenty minutes, with such earnestness! such conviction! such passion! such beauty. ... It was power in all its gentleness. He is a very great man.

— The Life of Mary Russell Mitford
edited by the Rev. A. G. K. L'Estrange
(2 vols., 1870), II, 272

Bring me my bow of burning gold!
   Bring me my arrows of desire!
Bring me my spear! O clouds, unfold!
   Bring me my chariot of fire!

I will not cease from mental fight,
   Nor shall my sword sleep in my hand,
Till we have built Jerusalem
   In England's green and pleasant land.

— From *Milton* by William Blake (1757–1827)

To the memory of my mother and father

ELIZABETH AND CHARLES HARTLEY

CHAPTER 1

Kingsley and F. D. Maurice

In the middle years of the nineteenth century Charles Kingsley, incumbent of St. Mary's parish church, Eversley, Hampshire, diverted his pen from drama to fiction, leaving six distinctive and highly unusual novels. A poetic piece in five acts, *The Saint's Tragedy* had come out early in 1848, but in July the first instalment of 'Yeast, or the Thoughts, Sayings, and Doings of Lancelot Smith, Gentleman' appeared anonymously in *Fraser's Magazine*, and both the title and the tenor of the piece indicated that the author was writing fiction. *Alton Locke* burst upon the scene in August, 1850, and *Yeast*, expanded into a book, followed in 1851. Then, *Hypatia* (1853), *Westward Ho!* (1855), and *Two Years Ago* (1857) came with relentless biennial regularity and, finally, after its serialization in *Good Words* during the whole of 1865, *Hereward the Wake* was published in the following year so that, with the exception of this work, Kingsley's novels all appeared within a single decade.

These novels were widely read, and for many years, by popular demand edition followed edition in seemingly endless succession. At the time of Kingsley's death in 1875 they adorned every household, and his name, like that of Queen Victoria, was equally indicative of the then great and far-flung Empire. Largely neglected today, Kingsley's novels are nevertheless representatively Victorian and are central to that period of swift change which occurred between 1845 and 1870.[1]

For this reason alone they should be looked at again. But as literary biographies they tell us much about the representative man who wrote them, and as the core of his work they are indicative of his thought in its best and most artistic form. Most importantly, as popular transcriptions of the theology of Frederick Denison Maurice (1805–72), they make a unique contribution to the religious outlook of the time. Kingsley's immediate purpose in writing his novels was to promote a political movement intended on the one

[1]

hand to rouse the governing classes to social action, and on the other to replace the bitterness in Chartism with Christian charity. Few other novels current at the time succeeded so well in bringing Christianity to the market-place, in urging the Ten Commandments, the Lord's Prayer, and the Sermon on the Mount as practical guides for men in a workaday world, and it is safe to say that none roused such contagious intensity of feeling. The novels represent Charles Kingsley's contribution to the Christian Social Movement, and they ought now to be read in conjunction with Kingsley's other writings.

The twenty-eight volumes of Kingsley's *Works* (1880–5) stand in order upon the shelf.[2] Many of the volumes have been read again and again, but all of them are now covered with dust and as a shaft of sunlight falls across their spines, the gold-lettered titles stand out on the faded blue of their bindings. There are sermons on the Gospels, on David, and on discipline; and other volumes announce *Sermons for the Times*, *Sermons on National Subjects*, and sermons preached by their author in Westminster Abbey, while still others indicate more sermons that were orated in village, town, and country. There are also volumes of lectures and essays, and judging from their titles, these treat subjects scientific and sanitary, social and historical. *Poems* is the first volume in the canon, while *Prose Idylls* appears half-way along the set. There are also the juvenile works for which Kingsley is generally remembered – *The Heroes*, the ever-popular *Water Babies*, and *Madam How and Lady Why*. But dispersed among these titles, also in their proper order, stand Kingsley's six novels, and we take the first of them from the shelf.

Yeast is an odd title for a book, but it is teasingly unusual, and as we thumb through the yellowed pages we come upon a fox-hunt in Hampshire:

The walk became a trot – the trot a canter. Then a faint melancholy shout at a distance, answered by a 'Stole away!' from the fields; a doleful 'toot!' of the horn; the dull thunder of many horsehoofs rolling along the further woodside. Then red coats, flashing like sparks of fire across the gray gap of mist at the ride's mouth. . . .

It is like seeing an aquatint on the stairs, and we continue to read at random:

. . . on and on – down the wind and down the vale; and the canter became a gallop, and the gallop a long straining stride; and a hundred horse-hoofs crackled like flame among the stubble, and thundered fetlock-deep along the heavy meadows; and every fence thinned the cavalcade, till the madness began to stir all bloods, and with grim earnest faces, the initiated few settled themselves to their work. . . . They crossed the stream, passed the Priory Shrubberies, leapt the gate into the park, and then on and upward, called by the unseen Ariel's music before them. – Up, into the hills, past white crumbling chalk-pits, . . . black fir-woods and silver beech, and here and there a huge yew standing out alone, . . .[3]

Indeed, it is like seeing a whole set of prints, each more exciting than the one before; and as we replace the book we make a mental note to return to it again.

Alton Locke is another world. Here is the work-room where Alton is joining the 'sweated' tailors:

. . . we emerged through a trap-door into a garret at the top of the house. . . . A low lean-to room, stifling me with the combined odours of human breath and perspiration, stale beer, the sweet sickly smell of gin, and the sour and hardly less disgusting one of new cloth. On the floor thick with dust and dirt, scraps of stuff and ends of thread, sat some dozen haggard, untidy, shoeless men, with a mingled look of care and recklessness. . . . The windows were tight closed to keep out the cold winter air; and the condensed breath ran in streams down the panes, chequering the dreary out-look of chimney-tops and smoke.[4]

A commentary on labour conditions among the London artisans, this book is a timely reminder of the evils that gave rise to Chartism, and it cannot be ignored.

Next comes *Hypatia*, and as we turn the worn pages our eyes light upon a gorgeous spectacle in an Alexandrian theatre:

The folding doors of the temple opened slowly; the crash of instruments resounded from within; and, preceded by the musicians came forth the triumph of Aphrodite, and passed down the slope, and down the outer ring of the orchestra.

A splendid car, drawn by white oxen, bore the rarest and gaudiest of foreign flowers and fruits, which young girls, dressed as Hours and Seasons, strewed in front of the procession and among the spectators.

A long line of beautiful youths and maidens, crowned with garlands, and robed in scarfs of purple gauze, followed by two and two. Each pair carried or led a pair of wild animals, captives of the conquering might of beauty.

Foremost were borne, on the wrists of the actors, the birds especially sacred to the goddess – . . .

Then followed strange birds from India, parakeets, peacocks, pheasants, silver and golden; bustards and ostriches: the latter bestridden each by a tiny cupid, were led in on golden leashes, followed by antelopes and oryxes, elks from beyond the Danube, four-horned rams from the Isles of the Hyperborean Ocean, and the strange hybrid of the Libyan hills believed by all the spectators to be half-bull, half-horse. And then a murmur of delighted awe ran through the theatre, as bears and leopards, lions and tigers, fettered in heavy chains of gold, and made gentle for the occasion by narcotics, paced sedately down the slope, obedient to their beautiful guides. . . .

A cry arose of 'Orestes! Orestes! Health to the illustrious Prefect! Thanks for his bounty!' . . .[5]

This is vivid and dramatic; but here is a sunrise on the Nile:

. . . a long arrow of level light flashed down the gorge from crag to crag, awakening every crack and slab to vividness and life. The great crimson sun rose swiftly through the dim night-mist of the desert, and as he poured his glory down the glen, the haze rose in threads and plumes, and vanished, leaving the stream to sparkle round the rocks, like the living, twinkling eye of the whole scene. Swallows flashed by hundreds out of the cliffs, and began their air-dance for the day; the jerboa hopped stealthily homeward on his stilts from his stolen meal in the monastery garden; the brown sand-lizards underneath the stones opened one eyelid each, and having satisfied themselves that it was day, dragged their bloated bodies and whip-like tails out into the most burning patch of gravel which they could find, and nestling together as a further protection against the cold, fell fast asleep again; the buzzard, who considered himself the lord of the valley, awoke with a long querulous bark, and rising aloft in two or three vast rings, to stretch himself after his night's sleep, hung motionless, watching every lark which chirruped on the cliffs; while from the far-off Nile below, the awakening croak of pelicans, the clang of geese, the whistle of the godwit and curlew, came ringing up the windings of the glen; and last of all the voices of the monks rose chanting a morning hymn to some wild Eastern air; and a new day had begun in Scetis, . . .[6]

Replacing *Hypatia*, we have mixed feelings as our eyes fall upon *Westward Ho!* But we restrain an impulse to take it down, for we know it well. We are familiar with Kingsley's treatment of the spacious days of good Queen Bess, of Francis Drake and Hawkins, of Raleigh and Richard Grenville; and we leave it for a more leisurely time.

Two Years Ago speaks of cholera and the Crimea. But we had forgotten how powerfully Kingsley personified the scourge:

He had come at last, Baalzebub, God of flies, and of what flies are bred from; to visit his self-blind worshippers, and bestow on them his own Cross of the Legion of Dishonour. He had come suddenly, capriously, sportively, as he sometimes comes . . . with appetite more fierce than ever, and had darted aside to seize on Aberalva, and not to let it go till he had sucked his fill. . . . And up and down the foul fiend sported, now here now there; snapping daintily at unexpected victims, as if to make confusion worse confounded. . . . He had taken old Beer's second son; and now he clutches at the old man himself; then across the street to Gentleman Jan, his eldest. . . .[7]

How remote from Elizabeth's jaunty sailors is this!

Hereward the Wake, in turn, kindles the imagination as much as Kingsley's Elizabethan tale. It transports us into a world of saga and myth, and passages like the following fill us with pleasurable melancholy as we read of the wide fens in eleventh-century England. 'Even now', writes Kingsley, 'they have a beauty of their own –

a beauty as of the sea, of boundless expanse and freedom. Much more had they that beauty eight hundred years ago, when they were still, for the most part, as God had made them, or rather was making them even then. The low rolling uplands were clothed in primaeval forest; oak and ash, beech and elm, . . . Always, from the foot of the wolds, the green fields stretched away, illimitable, to an horizon where, from the roundness of the earth, the distant trees and islands were hulled down like ships at sea. . . . Overhead the arch of heaven spread more ample than elsewhere. . . .'[8]

These novels are anything but dull, for they display considerable variety, not only in narrative treatment, but in background and scenic setting as well: a fox-hunt in Hampshire and a 'sweated' tailors' work-room in London; an Alexandrian theatre in 415; Devon and the Armada in 1588; cholera and the Crimea in the 1850s; and the English world of 1066 – here is epic scope indeed. But each novel clearly sprang from the particular context of a unique set of circumstances to which the characters are made to respond in accordance with the inner springs of their beings, and each novel, it would seem, is an artistic unity intended by the author to portray human beings in characteristic representational responses to daily life as practised at widely differing points in time and place. Each, then, becomes a finished portrait painted to illustrate Charles Kingsley's reading of life, and each must therefore be examined for itself as a vital illustration of the message that Kingsley sought to impart.

Yet, in spite of their individual colour and variety, when the six novels are looked at as a whole conveying the author's total view of human activity, they convey an epic panorama ranging over more than a thousand years of history; and one senses that their greatest value may lie in their illustration of Kingsley's belief that genuine history was no more than a record of the 'virtues and vices' of human beings in their responses to the age-old dictates for human behaviour set forth in the Commandments.[9]

From an artistic view-point these novels are obviously of considerable merit. The strong narrative line sustained by suspense, the smooth-flowing periods, the sweeping style and cumulative detail in paragraph-building and, above all, the splendid descriptions all suggest an author who, though hardly in the first rank of novelists, is yet one possessed of great gifts. Surface flaws apart, there is much fine writing which is distinguished for its precise diction and cutting felicity of phrase, that reveals great skill in the use of language. The vivid and poetic descriptions of landscape, whether wild or pastoral, and the bold strokes in which the canvases are drawn proclaim a literary genius, whose nature was exceptionally imaginative and undeniably facile in the use of the pen.

What manner of man, then, was Charles Kingsley? Since each novel inevitably reveals something of its author, a knowledge of the factors shaping Kingsley's life must supplement the study of the novels themselves. The nature of Maurice's influence and Kingsley's reasons for writing have already been briefly indicated. But what, besides novel-writing, were his interests and activities? What were the elements in his background supplying the guiding principles in his life, and what manner of man was he? Answers to these questions must clarify our picture of the man himself as well as enlarging the hints already given for his fictional activities.

Charles Kingsley was born on 12 June, 1819, at Holne in Devonshire.[10] When he was five years old his family removed to Barnack near Peterborough on the edge of the fen country, and here he lived until his eleventh year when the family returned to Devon and settled at Clovelly where his father had been presented to the living. Devon thus became his home for a second time, and here he remained until 1836 when 'the happy free country life' was exchanged for London and his father's rectory at St. Luke's, Chelsea. In London he attended King's College before going up to Magdalene College, Cambridge, in 1838.

During the decade following the Bristol Riots in 1831, while Charles was still a student, first at Helston Grammar School under the Rev. Derwent Coleridge, then at King's College and, afterwards, at Magdalene, the state of the country and of his mind presented similar and unpredictable parallels. Though Peterloo massacres and Bristol riots were short crises in a rising tide of discontent, both augured the overthrow of established authority by revolutionary forces similar to those toppling thrones in Europe. Mingling social ills with his own problems, Kingsley, like his country, alternated between moods of excitement and depression, and his life at Cambridge was especially marked first, by debauchery, then, by mental and spiritual conflicts and, finally, by a religious conversion. His regeneration is fictionalized in *Yeast*.

He had met his future wife, Miss Frances Eliza Grenfell, on 6 July, 1839, and they had married on 10 January, 1844. During the long courtship each of them had experienced a religious conversion in which each regarded the other as the principal agent. Miss Grenfell – Fanny, Kingsley called her – had guided Charles's reading by sending him the works of Coleridge, Carlyle, and Maurice. Through her influence and their writings he had gradually become convinced that he had a vocation in the Church. On his twenty-second birthday he had sent her a note to say that 'before the sleeping earth and the sleepless sea and stars' he had made a vow to devote himself to God.

In 1842, at Miss Grenfell's request, he had taken up *The Kingdom of Christ*[11] and, *mirabile dictu*, the vision had burst upon him. He 'saw God and Christ when he was twenty-three', his wife told a friend many years later,[12] and Kingsley's letters to Miss Grenfell between 1842 and 1844, when he married her and met Maurice, sing with a new note of assurance and joy. 'I seem all spirit', he wrote, 'and my every nerve is a musical chord trembling in the wind!' Amid much talk of brotherhood and collective humanity there are frequent references to God as a Father, to Christ as the Ideal Man, who 'used the earth' for man's sake, and to the Church as a human Family. Every creature of God is good and 'all world-generations have but one voice!'

... the trees and the flowers and birds, and the motes of rack floating in the sky, seem to cry to me: 'Thou knowest us! Thou knowest we have a meaning, and sing a heaven's harmony by night and day! Do us justice!...
And every man's and woman's eyes too, ... they cry to me through dim and misty strugglings: 'Oh do us justice! ... How can we become One? at harmony with God and God's universe! ... We shall see God! ... and be ready to wait for the renewal, for the Kingdom of Christ perfected![13]

The year 1844 was the most auspicious in his career. He and his bride settled at the rectory in Eversley, where he remained for the rest of his life. But although she had put him on the road and guided him in the way, to Maurice he owed the final light of all his seeing, and he was naturally anxious to meet the man whose writings had influenced him so greatly.

In July, he made bold to introduce himself. He excused himself for presuming to write to a comparative stranger on the ground that as a young priest he had no alternative but to seek advice from 'the elder prophet'. 'To your works', he wrote Maurice, 'I am indebted for the foundation of any coherent view of the word of God, the meaning of the Church of England, and the spiritual phenomena of the present and past ages'.[14] Maurice's liberal theology was already a bond between them, and Kingsley's letter anticipated their close association in the Christian Social Movement that they and John Malcolm Forbes Ludlow were to initiate in 1848.

Kingsley's declaration became an intensely serious commitment, and in entrusting himself to Maurice he was surrendering himself to one whom he regarded as a prophet. His confidence included not only the Bible and the Church, but Maurice's theology and his philosophy of history as well. It seemed foreordained that he was to be Maurice's spokesman. It was enough for him, he said, to be 'the interpreter of Maurice to the outside world',[15] and he did so in sermon, song, and novel from this time forward. As we shall see, the *raison d'être* for his fiction became the dramatization of the theological principles enunciated by Maurice, the very same, indeed, that lay behind his own vocation in the Church, when Maurice became 'the Master'.

On the threshold of his career, then, Kingsley had been most deeply moulded by two people – his wife, and Frederick Denison Maurice. If prior to their marriage Miss Grenfell had guided his reading, her role as his wife now became that of a perceptive and deeply appreciative helpmate. Because of the tender domesticity of the rectory over which she presided, much of the restless excitability that had characterized his youth and early manhood seemed to vanish. He had always regarded woman as the civilizer of man, and the measure of balance and stability that Mrs. Kingsley gave her husband made his theory emphatically the corner-stone of his philosophy. 'To his wife – he owed the whole tenor of his life, all that he had worth living for'[16] and without her, he would have accomplished little.

Indirectly, he owed his acquaintance with Maurice to her, and the rich and enduring friendship that grew out of their meeting complemented hers in his life. In their exchange of visits, in their copious correspondence, and in their close association in working for reform Kingsley came to know and understand his mentor as few other men did. It was Maurice who made him see that 'Thy kingdom come', which he daily prayed, was the sum of his mission. Not only in his parish as his particular field of labour, but in the whole kingdom of England, the kingdom of Christ was to be renewed and extended.

Maurice conceived social reformation to begin with a re-assertion of the Trinity. God had established 'an actual covenant with humanity in Christ', our Elder Brother, and the covenant was 'the actual foundation of the universe, the ground of a Divine and human family', because it depended on 'absolute Fatherly Love'. In a Christian country this is implied in the rite of baptism, Maurice had pointed out, and in his third *Tract on Christian Socialism* (1850),[17] where he explained the connexion between Christian socialism and the Church, he told the clergy that they were to accept the poor as their brothers because they were God's children. Human relations on earth were to emulate the Spirit of Love existing between the Father, our Father, and the Son, our Brother; and this was the sum of Christian socialism.

His views on the Trinity are elaborated in the *Kingdom of Christ*, and Mrs. Kingsley was to name this as the book to which her husband owed most. 'By it his views were cleared and his faith established', she declared,[18] and Kingsley corroborated this in a letter to Thomas Cooper in 1857.[19] Perhaps the most important concept in Maurice's treatise apart from that on the Trinity itself as the foundation of society,[20] is his exposition of the relation between the human conscience and the Trinitarian God. Nineteenth-century theology prior to Maurice had stressed man as the fallen Adam ever vulnerable to eternal damnation, whereas Maurice re-affirmed Christ, the New Man, as the representative of humanity, its Saviour and Redeemer.

Moral and Metaphysical Philosophy (1872), another basic work of Maurice's, and one which he first outlined in *The Encyclopaedia Metropolitana* (1839-40) and expanded and published sectionally at intervals during his lifetime, revealed the Bible as a history unfolding God's ways to man. Far from contradicting pagan records, the Bible explains them in a manner that makes the New Dispensation a natural sequel to the Old, and designates the way in which latter-day man can continue with the building of God's kingdom on earth. The *Philosophy* also expounds the meaning of society and defines conscience as an unfailing guide to action; and on the information in this treatise Kingsley erected his own philosophy of history.[21]

Between the appearance of the *Saint's Tragedy* in 1848 and the publication of *Yeast* in 1851 occurred the events that rushed Kingsley into novel-writing, and these will be outlined in the next chapter. And just as the mind of Maurice was to guide the initial activities in the Christian Social Movement so, as Kingsley freely appropriated his mentor's ideas, was that mind to light every page of those novels: the family as the nucleus of society; human as imaging divine relationships; the freedom of a will that paradoxically acts in obedience to God; conscience as man's infallible guide; the insistence that the contemporary view of eternal punishment distorted Christ's teaching and drove many to 'the devil's side'; truth as residual in the reconciliation of polarities; the Kingdom of Christ as a living, growing organism, and religious conversion as the effective means of renewing society and furthering that Kingdom – all these ideas Kingsley was to pass on from Maurice in novels that caught the popular imagination and went a long way toward re-directing mid-nineteenth-century society into happier, more equitable paths.

Possessed of Maurice's social ideas, Kingsley had much to say and a burning desire to say it; and again, it was Maurice who instructed him on the nature of literature. Maurice had theories about language, about the nature and character of the writer, and about the meaning of literature in national history; and these stimulated Kingsley quite as much as Maurice's explanations of theology had done.

Language was the distinctive sign of humanity.[22] As an organ of communication, it was also the means to relationships, and history is a record of human relations contradistinguished from those in nature. Once men had developed a language for the transmission of relationships, that language became the instrument by which human society could itself develop and cohere, and the national literature expressed a characteristic social policy. Literature and society were parts of each other, and since they had grown out of relationships, an ethical code of behaviour inevitably unfolded as well. Broadly speaking, literature and theology were one.

With the development of language, personality became the 'crowning blossom of creation'[23] and, because of his facility with words, the man of letters inevitably became a leading figure. Maurice declared poetry, the highest form of literature, to be 'contemporaneous with the commencement of orderly and coherent language', and thus he made the poet – the writer – instrumental in uniting persons of the same tongue:

The periods in which the bonds of political union have been most strongly realized, are those in which poetry has manifested itself in its greatest power. . . . It is exactly in that communion between men, which exists in a political body circumscribed by definite limits, that each man vividly and consciously realizes his relation to the whole, and rises through the sense of that relation to the dignity of a personal being; and of these feelings poetry seems to be the legitimate and intended expression. The crisis of deliverance is that which gives occasion to its utterance: one person, who most strongly feels that he is a member of the nation, expresses by words the excited feeling of his own spirit, and those words married to music are felt by the whole society as their own.[24]

The 'one person', the poet, not only expressed his thoughts as the thoughts of all, but in doing so he made 'the political body circumscribed by definite limits' a nation, and thus bound the members of it together. But although his 'expressed words' – his poetry – gave him distinction and made him a kind of hero, he was none the less keenly aware that he owed his position to the national group itself. Each particular event in his nation's development needed him to be its spokesman, and it was his solemn duty to be so. Like Carlyle, Maurice believed that in times of national crisis a man who was exceptionally gifted in the use of language arose 'to expound the principles of the Divine government', and thus to bring out the moral order applicable to it. As the ages passed revealing new aspects of God's purposes, new prophets arose to interpret the eternal message afresh.

The poet was by nature a prophet, and in the spirit of the Hebraic language of the Old Testament which uses one word for both offices, Maurice saw the poet as guiding 'the rulers of states and the chief of hosts'. Isaiah, for example, had observed the events of his day, had 'contemplated them *in idea* as they were in themselves', and had then proclaimed them in preaching and writing as 'the Counsels of God'.[25] In him as in all prophets extremes had met: both hero and servant, he was also a recluse and a statesman. As the former, he had lived 'in the most awful and mysterious contemplation' while, as the latter, his contemplations had borne significantly on the 'ordinary transactions of life'.[26]

The poet thus wore a mantle of awful responsibility. He enunciated 'the meaning and spirit of the Divine law'. He showed how 'the ignorance and transgressions of rulers, priests, and people lead to national ruin', and he proclaimed 'a great moral order in the world' for general guidance in preserving the nation against decay since, above all, he carried men into a region above positive law, into the deep and inward principles of law, into their connections with the heart of man, into their effect upon his affections.

Since society was neither 'a machine moving by an impulse communicated to it at creation', nor a body directed by the caprices of the human will, the poet had unceasingly to remind his countrymen that the 'continual progress' of the moral order was superintended by a Living Person.

Though this was the acknowledged role of the Biblical prophet, it seemed somehow less acceptable for the modern writer. By its own telling, however, the nineteenth century was an age of prophets, and Maurice again made the concept powerfully applicable. The Lord and Giver of Light had inspired all men, he said, and the prophet differed from ordinary men only in his heightened receptivity to revelation, which gave him an almost unbearable sense of power. But Maurice went on to explain in *The Epistle to the Hebrews* (1846) that every 'true teacher' received these 'divine communications', and in as much as he was indeed God's messenger he had to yield to them, although he was unable to speak until the energizing force had made him humbly aware that his words, though coming from the depths of his own heart, came indeed from God, and belonged to his countrymen as to himself.

Possessed of these ideas, Kingsley saw the writer in a new and glorious light. The prophets of the Old Testament who had written with authority and conviction were but men like Socrates and Plato, and all of them had testified to eternal truth. Moreover, Maurice, like Carlyle, was a recognized prophet in his day and generation, while Kingsley himself was undeniably a poet of the humbler sort. More importantly, however, as a clergyman whose avowed vocation was the preaching of the Gospel, he had inevitably taken on the mantle of those prophets and, this being so, could he as a lesser prophet do better than endeavour to speak for the greater? Among his acquaintances Maurice was the friend most deeply imbued with the wisdom of the ages, and in trying to interpret him, would he not indeed be emulating the work of the prophets – indeed, of Jesus, that meek poet-prophet who, during his brief lifetime on earth, used those nearest to him in making his testimony to Truth?

But thirdly, Maurice instructed his disciple more particularly in the meaning of national literature. Because it was *the* European country which, for all moral and political purposes, had begun its history simultaneously with that of the Christian era itself, Maurice saw the island of Britain as a 'specimen' nation illustrative of Christian civilization. His lectures on the ecclesiastical history of the first two centuries of the Christian era reflect the tone and spirit of those he gave at King's College on English literature, for both series unfolded the gradual establishment of the Kingdom of Christ in the world. In these lectures he threw the diverse aspects of nineteenth-century society back upon the nucleus of Christian society and, by returning to the beginning, he could make contemporary society see itself beside that mirrored in English literature. Thus did he impress upon his readers the impact of history upon their 'present', and thus did he relate contemporary political events to the whole range of the past and in this way teach them that English literature embodied an ideal illustration of the developing Christian nation.

Development was a matter of process, and among other things he stressed the historical struggle to be seen in that literature between right and wrong tendencies in the growing society. He saw the first Christians as having fostered a system of their own devising rather than Christ's commonwealth. Certain leading-men, he thought, had early begun to replace the teaching of Jesus about the Kingdom, which was based on His Father's will, with a christian religion, and thus to substitute their *hierarchy* for His *polity*.[27] Human system-building had arisen because man was prone to make himself his own centre, and as it had been in the beginning so it was in nineteenth-century England. The struggle between good and evil, between self-sacrifice and selfishness, runs through the annals of history, and English literature becomes a transcript of English society testifying to the fact. From the tenuous relationships of the Canterbury pilgrims to Wordsworth and Coleridge in Maurice's own day the theme is ever-present in English literature; and Kingsley was soon to write *Hypatia* to portray the conflict in fifth-century Alexandria, while *Westward Ho!* and *Hereward the Wake* were to delineate the same conflicts, respectively, in eleventh- and sixteenth-century England, the more effectively to alert his own generation to the continuing struggle among themselves.

Finally, Maurice's definition of the conscience as a 'feeling' prepared the way, both for the union between the poet and his poetry, and between his poetry and his nation. Poetry, Maurice asserted, surpassed the mere feeling of unity by lifting men to 'the contemplation of truth and goodness'. The assimilation of these, he declared, went beyond mere national enthusiasm to the perception of an 'intimate fellowship with a Being above' as well as a similar one with those beings around us. Poetry testified to 'a universal society' founded on 'truth and goodness', whose life is 'order and harmony'. And finally, since

the existence of the individual and of society are alike based upon the idea of justice, and are alike sustained by the contemplation of that which is true and permanent, and alike die a moral death when they contradict the principles of their being,

poetry unites man with God and witnesses to immortality.[28]

These ideas, too, caught Kingsley's imagination. The romance of an organic Christian society in continuous growth for eighteen centuries lit his mind with the same bright vision that Maurice's fresh marriage of the poet with the prophet had done. Now as never before he saw that there was an irrefutable brotherhood between man and man, and an equally indisputable communion between man and God, with poetry as the means and a Father in heaven as the all-embracing Unifier. Kingsley's excited feelings knew no bounds and, as Canon Raven has summarized, if Maurice was the Moses of the Christian Social Movement, Kingsley 'with his power of tongue and pen' was certainly its Aaron.

Believing poetry to combine painting, music, and history,[29] Kingsley saw his task clearly before him. The art of his time needed a poet who could sing about common things concerning all men in a language that all could understand. There was Maurice as a recognized prophet whom he felt compelled to popularize, and he had some ability for doing so, as *The Saint's Tragedy* attested. As for his age, it differed as much from that of Shakespeare as he himself differed from the bard. 'Heroic himself', Shakespeare had lived in 'an age of heroes', and Kingsley believed it to have been the continual presence of these heroes together with the atmosphere of 'respect and trust' in which Shakespeare had lived, that had tamed 'the wild selfwill of the deer-stealing fugitive from Stratford into the calm large-eyed philosopher', who had shown 'faith in a species made in the likeness of God'.[30] And these same heroes had also shown him the nature of history, for, as Maurice had said, Shakespeare

found in the chronicles and tales which he read, men of all degrees, ages, and countries, who, because he took them to be essentially of the same flesh and blood and to have the same life with those whom he met in the streets and taverns, presented themselves to him, and through him in a degree to us, with an awful distinctness; so that we know that they *were*, and cannot but feel that they *are*.[31]

Keenly aware that he was no Shakespeare, but also familiar with old chronicles and tales, Kingsley tremblingly took up his pen. Mightier than the sword, it was also further-reaching than the voice of the preacher. Kingsley had long since been expressing himself in sermons which, like his periodical writings, were red-hot with the glow of spiritual passion, and since these had been written before being preached, poetry and fiction of a similar order followed as a matter of course.

As might be expected, Kingsley's style sometimes resembles that of the Old Testament prophets. The Hebrew poet perceived by feeling and, as Herder remarked in *The Spirit of Hebrew Poetry*, he 'told in song what he felt'. It is this quality of perceptive feeling that strengthens Kingsley's affinity with them in his written work. Biblical writers were always less concerned with the creation of literary forms than with graphic expression calculated to stimulate the emotions and move readers to action, and Kingsley's style is remarkable for the same quality. He wrote with impulsive energy, with a burning intensity for the need of the hour and, impregnated with Maurice's ideas, at his best he is persuasively appealing.

Though Kingsley's view of history will emerge in the analyses of his novels, it may be said in passing that Coleridge gave him a concept of history that, by way of Maurice, was to inform his fiction, particularly that denominated historical. In his *Lay Sermons*,

Coleridge described the Bible as a science of realities, and each of its elements as 'a living germ in which the present involves the future', so that 'in the finite the infinite exists potentially'. As we have seen, for Kingsley 'the only key' to the present was the past,[32] and since the finite present contains an infinite future, not only the Bible, but the printed page itself becomes a mediator presenting the past as a guide to the future; and for Kingsley, history was 'a picture of the spirits of our forefathers', a view amply illustrated in *Westward Ho!* and *Hereward the Wake.*

Kingsley believed that genius worked in him as the reflex of God's mind. The notion filled him with a burning enthusiasm, the expression of which he could not stem. More intensely for him than for most men, words represented purposes and ideas, and these were analogous to evolution and extension in the plant. Both were growing, and Kingsley saw metaphor as the means of language. Moreover, he considered it figurative for the poet but literal for the theologian.[33] Writing imaginatively, he could use the figure to body forth subjective symbols while, in religious work, he could use it literally. Like Maurice's Christian society, language was organic, and with the rising sun of Christianity both language and society had commenced their outward life; and in England they entered into open communion with all the elements of life, at once assimilating them to themselves and so to the polity at large.[34]

Accepting Coleridge and Maurice again, Kingsley regarded prose as the highest kind of poetry. Language had developed into what is commonly received as poetry because of a natural tendency for rhyme and rhythm. Employing 'a confined and arbitrary metre' and a periodic recurrence of sounds, poetry, these men thought, was gradually disappearing into higher forms like the drama and the novel, and was passing into prose of a 'free and ever-shifting flow of every imaginable rhythm and metre, determined by no arbitrary rules, but only by the spiritual intent of the subject'.[35] Kingsley had a flair for creating elevated and harmonious successions of sentences expressing a 'deliberate reason' while at one and the same time lifting the imagination aloft.

Kingsley's imagination was brilliant, almost haunted. During his youth he found it hard to distinguish between imagination and dream, and between imagination and waking impression. He was often thought to be 'romancing' when he was relating actual impressions, and under periods of stress he sometimes had spectral illusions accompanied with 'nervous excitability', which he controlled with salutary effect as he grew older. Maurice helped him to see that imagination had to act in accord with reason and, applying Coleridge's distinction between fancy and imagination, Kingsley excluded the former the better to exert a 'fearless honesty' in facing the social malaise around him.

It was the vividness of his imagination that drove him to an abiding interest in social amelioration. While he was an impressionable student of thirteen at the Old Kingswood School in Clifton, an unforgettable lesson was seared upon his mind even as it was written in 'letters of flame' against the thick smog that hovered over Bristol on a memorable Sunday afternoon in November, 1831. Rioters had set fire to Lawford's Gate prison and, drawn by the lurid glare that was visible through the autumn fog, Kingsley absorbed the weird blend of ugliness and beauty as the flames had risen higher and higher, 'not red alone,

but delicately green and blue, pale rose and pearly white, while crimson sparks leapt and fell again in the midst of that rainbow, not of hope but of despair; and dull explosions down below mingled with the roar of the mob, and the infernal hiss and crackle of the flame. Higher and higher the fog was scorched and shrivelled upward by the fierce heat below, glowing through and through with red reflected glare, . . .[36]

The physical facts supplied a moral analogue; and many years afterwards Kingsley recalled that beyond the lurid mass he could see far away the lonely tower of a village church, 'the symbol of the old faith, looking down in stately wonder and sorrow upon the fearful birth-pangs of a new age'.

Memorable as this scene had been, added to its awesome beauty some days later was the horror of seeing 'a ghastly row, not of corpses, but of corpse fragments', to one of which there adhered 'a scrap of old red petticoat'. The lesson was never to be forgotten. For a time, the experience made him 'the veriest aristocrat', full of hatred and contempt for those dangerous classes whose existence he had become aware of for the first time. It required many years of 'personal intercourse' with these people to teach him 'the true meaning' of what he had seen.[37]

Indeed, the incident made him a radical for a time. It led him to the assumption that 'all men are born into the world equals, and that their inequality . . . is chargeable entirely to circumstances'. He learned in the harsh school of experience, however, that there are 'congenital difference and hereditary tendencies which defy education from circumstances'. Almost thirty years later he was to affirm that society might pity those who were born 'fools or knaves' but that she could not, 'for her own sake', allow them power.[38] The poor were by no means either, but Kingsley's change in viewpoint marks the difference in attitude between *Alton Locke* and *Two Years Ago*.

Imagination also pricked his conscience in another way. It gave him insight into the lives of scapegraces or, as he himself chose to express it, 'sympathy with blackguards'. John Martineau reports that he had often seen Kingsley seat himself beside 'a tramp, on the grass' in order to hear the fellow's story.[39] Although his imagination operated in his historical writings to make the past vivid, it also coloured his contemporary novels as well, and this imaginative sympathy combined with his literary gifts to make him write what he had seen and heard with 'the free outpouring' of a truly vivid and living conception.[40]

Each of the novels thus becomes 'a flight outward from assimilated experience,' and none is more emphatically Charles Kingsley's signature than *Yeast*.[41] The Christian Social Movement precipitated Kingsley into novel-writing and *Yeast* was actually dashed off under the compelling necessity to record his 'good news' before he could settle down to other matters. It was his first novel because, for him, his personal conversion supplied the answer, not only for other troubled and doubting persons, but for the whole nation. It thus becomes a seminal novel, the theme and structure of which inform every other that he was to write.

Contrary to the opinions of many unwitting contemporary reviewers, Kingsley's novels are relatively strong in plot, largely because they are built on the phases in religious conversion. Kingsley naturally went to the Bible for models, and whether following the conversions of Old Testament figures like Moses and Isaiah, or that of Saul who became St. Paul of the New, all of them terminate in a mission to mankind. Isaiah, for example, saw the Lord on his throne. He was immediately convinced of the reality of his vision, then, of his own sin in the cry, 'Woe is me!'. When his lips were purged with a live coal and his sin thus removed, his mission offer followed at once: 'Here am I; send me'. William James also suggested the possibilities for plot in defining conversion as a 'process' by which a self 'hitherto divided, and consciously wrong . . . becomes unified and consciously right' owing to its 'firmer hold' upon religious reality.[42] Its most epic use occurs in the Biblical account of the conversion of the Israelites, where alternate turnings to and from Jehovah indicate the 'perpetual systole and diastole of the heart of Israel'.[43]

In general, Kingsley's characterization is weak. Whether in Alexandria, Devon, or the Isle of Ely his female characters tend to become incurably Victorian despite the period costumes in which he clothes them. Often they degenerate into sentimentality. Among his heroes there is little to choose between Tom Thurnall, Amyas Leigh, or Hereward, since all of them are rather like Spenser's knights in the *Faerie Queene* – indistinct as individuals but pointed and clear-cut in the actions which they represent. Morally, they develop or dwindle in stature in accordance with their achievement of, or decline from heroism.

But in spite of these general faults some of them are strongly portrayed, and Kingsley offers an interesting glimpse into his method of character portrayal in hints offered to a rising young protegé:

. . . when you talk of meeting the old fisherman – which fisherman? What fisherman? Why leave him as a mere ghost! Give the shape of his nose, the presence or absence of a pocket-handkerchief thereto, shape of his small clothes, tears in his coat, colour of the hand which took the baccy, twist of the mouth with which he deposited it in his toothless jaw, etc., etc., and you have a live man, not an abstract thing. Define him as you saw him, . . . 'He looked primitive'; wherein? What made his 'primitiveness'? Expound forthwith.

He has followed his own precepts in his drawing of Harry Verney, 'a patriarch among all the game-keepers of the vale', in *Yeast*:

F. D. MAURICE

National Portrait Gallery, London

He was a short, wiry, bandy-legged, ferret-visaged old man, with grizzled hair and a wizened face, tanned brown and purple by constant exposure. Between rheumatism and constant handling the rod and gun, his fingers were crooked like a hawk's claws. He kept his left eye always shut, apparently to save trouble in shooting; and squinted and sniffed, and peered, with a stooping back and protruded chin, as if he were perpetually on the watch for fish, flesh, and fowl, vermin and Christian. The friendship between himself and the Scotch terrier at his heels would have been easily explained by Lessing, for in the transmigration of souls the spirit of Harry Verney had evidently once animated a dog of that breed. He was dressed in a huge thick fustian jacket, scratched, stained, and patched, with bulging, greasy pockets; a cast of flies round a battered hat, riddled with shot-holes, a dog whistle in his buttonhole, and an old gun cut short over his arm, bespoke his business.[44]

Unexcelled in the art of description, Kingsley also revealed the secret of his power to the same protegé:

Set to work as in a picture, putting in your sky and background first, then sketching the general form and colour of your object, then working it up minutely, even to every moss upon the rock (as far as you really would or did see where you stood), and then finish off with some foreground connecting it with you or with some individual definition of what made it in your eyes *that* place and no other. ... And in this you will find the immense value of varied general knowledge. It gives you a power of illustration, endless analogies, association on association, which is the very charm of this [?] writing; and which, and all the rest, you will find, by the bye, better than anywhere in Christopher North's *Recreations*. ... Thus you will fulfill your promise to the reader by showing him how much *you* saw (and he will take for granted, trust him, that he would have seen it all just as well had he been there). Whereas you have a little deceived yourself, by forgetting that the names which call up pictures in your memory do not do so in his, and that you must draw them for him.[45]

The novels abound in descriptions built upon this principle, but in *Hereward the Wake* is one that is done, equally effectively, in reverse. As Hereward and Lady Godiva row away to Crowland in the barge taking his dead brother to the Abbey for burial, we follow them

by many a mere and many an ea; through narrow reaches of clear brown glassy water; between the dark-green alders; between the pale-green reeds; where the coot clanked, and the bittern boomed, and the sedge-bird, not content with its own sweet song, mocked the notes of all the birds around; and then out into the broad lagoons, where hung motion-less, high over head, hawk beyond hawk, buzzard beyond buzzard, kite beyond kite, as far as eye could see. Into the air, as they rowed on, whirred up great skeins of wild fowl innumerable, with a cry as of all the bells of Crowland, or all the hounds of the Bruneswald; while clear above all their noise sounded the wild whistle of the curlews, and the trumpet note of the great white swan.[46]

The reader remains with the figures in the foreground, but as the barge drifts on, the picture grows – forward and outward to Crow-land, to the Bruneswald, and to high heaven itself, in the 'trumpet note of the great white swan'.

Equally graphic, but arousing very different feelings is this description of St. Giles's on 'a foul, chilly, Saturday night' with its houses 'piled up into the dingy night' and 'hanging like cliffs' over Clare Market. Suggestive of Tom-All-Alone's in *Bleak House*, Kingsley describes the 'hell on earth', the 'brawling torrents of filth, and poverty, and sin' characteristic of London's Victorian poor:

From the butchers' and greengrocers' shops the gas lights flared and flickered, wild and ghastly, over haggard groups of slip-shod dirty women, bargaining for scraps of stale meat and frost-bitten vegetables, wrangling about short weight and bad quality. Fish-stalls and fruit-stalls lined the edge of the greasy pavement, sending up odours as foul as the language of sellers and buyers. Blood and sewer-water crawled from under doors and out of spouts, and reeked down the gutters among offal, animal and vegetable, in every stage of putrefaction. Foul vapours rose from cowsheds and slaughter houses, and the door-ways of undrained alleys, where the inhabitants carried the filth out on their shoes from the back-yard into the court, and from the court up into the main street.[47]

Nor are the novels lacking in pathos. Few can read 'How Amyas Came Home the Third Time' (Ch. XXVIII) without feeling a lump in the throat. Kingsley uses sharp contrast to heighten suspense and rouse deep-felt emotion. In the midst of their revelry marking the end of Catholic rule, the jubilant townsfolk, suddenly sobered by a 'flash' and 'the thunder of a gun at sea', chill at the thought of Spanish reprisals. As a galleon approaches the harbour-bar fear strikes every heart, then quickly mingles with expectancy for, Spanish though she is, she has never 'veiled her topsails' and there is 'music on board'. As she opens 'full on Burrough House' cheers burst from her crew, and roll up to the hills. The hushed spectators cannot know that Amyas now pilots this very galleon bursting with Spanish gold – the spoils of his company's heroic victory at sea.

But his mother does. The frail and pious lady at Burrough House, who knows intuitively that she has lost one son to the Inquisition and has been awaiting Amyas's return these three years, calmly informs her maid, 'Master Amyas is come home!' Suddenly the whole town is throbbing with excitement and renewed jubilation. But there is no mistaking the role of womanhood in the making of heroes. Their hero has come home, but to the hero's heroine goes the glory:

'Here she is!' shouted some one; 'here's his mother!' . . . The next moment the giant head and shoulders of Amyas, far above the crowd, swept round the corner.

'Make a way! Make room for Madam Leigh!' – And Amyas fell on his knees at her feet. She threw her arms round his neck, and bent her fair head over his, while sailors, 'prentices, and coarse harbour-women were hushed into holy silence, and made a ring round the mother and son.[48]

Kingsley's art speaks for itself. It must do so henceforth in this study, which is concerned more with the sermon than with the art that bodies it forth. This is as Kingsley himself had ordered it. Whatever we may think of his novels, it is but just to accept him on his own terms. Claiming no place in the literary world and insisting that he was a novelist only by accidents of time and place, he had little patience with art and valued his literary gifts but slightly. He was a writer, he said, because he was a clergyman about his Father's business: 'I am nothing if not a Priest', he once averred.[49] Maurice, who felt that no writer who believed 'the last and saddest crisis of his country's history' to be at hand, would trouble himself with the niceties of elegant composition except as he deemed them necessary for imparting truth and driving people to repentance, and these were Kingsley's sentiments as well. But it is now time to turn to the movement for which his novels were written.

CHAPTER 2

Parson Lot and Christian Socialism

Long before Kingsley's ordination in 1842, competition had
shattered the trust, affection, and respect that had characterized the
relationships between masters and their apprentices in the world of
labour. Moreover, this competitive spirit was fostered by an attitude
of *laissez-faire*, which strengthened the division of class from class
and Head from Hand. Competition was a terrible force breeding
alienation, envy, and mistrust. It had turned the country into a
'mere aggregation' of discontented and antagonistic individuals,[1]
and with the onslaught of the factory system society was falling apart.

Competition had precipitated a moral regression. The poor had
grown degenerate and fatalistic; the rich, covetous and irresponsible.
'God is my witness', Kingsley was to declare in a village sermon,
'one goes through some parts of England now, and sees . . . all the
sin and misery, and the people wearying themselves . . . for very
vanity . . .'[2] Tramps degraded in body, mind, and morals roamed
from parish to parish, begging, pilfering, and extorting money,
burning ricks and breaking into houses.[3] The rector of Frimley, a
parish but ten miles from Eversley, was murdered in his garden, and
several attempts were made on the rectory at Eversley, which had
perforce to be bolted and barred, the rector sleeping 'with loaded
pistols by his bedside'. In spite of this ominous but general state of
affairs, however, the middle and upper classes remained in a 'lap-
dog condition, in which comfort and dormant consciences made them
puppets of circumstance'.

Meanwhile, the workers had grown more demonstrative. Disillusioned with their masters, they were seeking self-government and
universal household suffrage. They had prepared, and were now
demanding, a six-point Charter of rights and when in March,
1848, France became a Republic, artisans everywhere grew threatening. In England under Feargus O'Connor their physical-force leader,
the working classes, many of whom were now Chartists, had planned

[24]

a great meeting on Kennington Common. April the 10th was the day set for a procession thence through London to Whitehall where, failing admission and a hearing, they planned to take 'less legal steps' to secure both.[4] As revolution seemed imminent the troops were called in and the principal buildings were garrisoned in preparation for the expected siege.

On Monday morning, 10 April, 1848, Charles Kingsley, Rector of Eversley and author of the recently published and controversial *Saint's Tragedy* came hurrying up to town to discuss the crisis with his friend and mentor who, as Chaplain of Lincoln's Inn, incumbent of two professorial chairs at King's College and author of *The Kingdom of Christ* (1838), was already in the forefront of ecclesiastical Liberalism. He was unable to accompany his discipline, but gave him an introduction to Ludlow. The French-trained barrister of Lincoln's Inn, who spoke several languages besides English and French, had returned from Paris not three weeks since, where the revolution had just occurred, and he had convinced Maurice of the need to Christianize the tide of socialism flooding into England from the Continent. Maurice's letter received and greetings exchanged, he and the excited Kingsley set out for Kennington Common, but they met the disconsolate Chartists on Waterloo Bridge. Though Feargus O'Connor had told them that 'he would head their procession' to parliament, he had also agreed to obey the authorities, and abandon it, so the 'honest father' had persuaded 'his children' to disperse.[5] As Kingsley was later to explain in *Alton Locke*, the meeting had broken up, 'drenched and cowed, body and soul, by pouring rain', while the gigantic petition, without its bannered coach-and-four, was cut into three, a ludicrous third put into each of three cabs, and hauled ignominiously away 'to be dragged to the floor of the House of Commons amid roars of laughter'. For the third time the Chartists' demands had ended in a fiasco.

The rain had continued, and as the London mists deepened into evening, Kingsley and Ludlow had returned to Maurice's house, where the three men considered ways of helping the Chartists in their humiliation. As they talked, the conviction came upon them that they were chosen instruments. The words of Christ at the beginning of His ministry came home to them as to one man:

The Spirit of the Lord is upon me, because He hath anointed me to preach the gospel to the poor; He hath set me to heal the broken-hearted, to preach deliverance to the captives, and recovering of sight to the blind; to set at liberty them that are bruised, to preach the acceptable year of the Lord (Luke IV: 16–21).

The Spirit upon Maurice, Ludlow, and Kingsley on that 10th day of April in that 'acceptable year of the Lord', was the same that had 'anointed' Christ to preach the gospel to the poor, and the founders of Christian Socialism, knowing their hour, began their task. Thus commenced that movement which history has recorded in the name that they gave it, Christian Socialism.

Before turning to the movement itself we may summarize the influences shaping Kingsley's social conscience. There was the environment in which he had grown up, and he contrasted the flat fens and the rocky Devonshire coast against which dashed the long Atlantic swell, and thus fed his imagination with delight.[6] Next, his father's rectory was naturally the local centre of social concerns, and like his father before him, Kingsley was now a clergyman facing familiar problems in his own parish. And if the elder Kingsley and his wife, 'a second Elizabeth Fry', were content to foster godliness and good living in the parish – most significantly for Charles, in the large but poor parish of St. Luke's, Chelsea – the younger Kingsley had a mission to reform society generally. His own conversion had given him a sense of urgency, and this had been fostered by the love and encouragement of his wife, whose conversion and attendant mission had merged with his own. But above all, there was *The Kingdom of Christ* and Maurice's liberal theology, together with the master's own warm friendship. Now, there was Christian Socialism as well.

While the movement was intended to culminate in practical associations of working men, the campaign of the founders was primarily literary and educative along theological lines. Each of the founders adopted a pseudonym and between 1848 and 1851 Kingsley, though sometimes remaining anonymous, usually wrote over the signature of Parson Lot. Of the work written by Kingsley during this time only *Yeast* and *Alton Locke* are fictional, and although these will be considered separately, we may note that they were both done in great excitement under the pressure of events at the start of the movement.

Parson Lot's other writings for the movement were frankly propagandist, and had little to do with the novels. But in them there emerged, not only in Parson Lot's work, but in Christian Socialist writings generally the necessary qualifications and distinctions in terminology, definition, and aim, that clarified Kingsley's purposes and gave him the positive assurance that he was to reveal in his novels. But not until he had finished *Alton Locke* was he clear about the way in which their purposes could best be achieved, and, as the sparks flew upward in the heat of the day, his zeal gradually abated, so that Parson Lot, who wrote in excitement and haste until 1851, was a more intense and fiery man than the later novelist, who wrote under his own name.

As we turn to the movement, then, we observe that Parson Lot was a man of strong feeling, impulsive in action, and bold in utterance. In 1848 Maurice was forty-three, Kingsley as Parson Lot, twenty-nine and in the prime of life with his best years all before him. Married to the woman who had led him into the Church, Rector of Eversley, and secure in his discipleship of Maurice, he bubbled with boyish enthusiasm and chafed for action. But he remained a man of strange contrasts. 'For all his man's strength', wrote John Martineau, 'there was a deep vein of *woman* in him, a nervous sensitiveness, an intensity of sympathy, which made him suffer when others suffered,' and this gave him an appeal that enabled him to elicit the inmost confidences of men and women in all walks of life.[7] Septimus Hansard also reported that he combined a feminine tenderness of feeling with an unyielding masculine strength of character, and this unusual combination intensified his awareness of the abominable social conditions of the time which, in turn, made it impossible for him to maintain 'the calm unruffled judgment'[8] of men less sensitive and less fiery in temperament. He always exercised strong self-control in an effort to reconcile these sharp contrasts, however, and in this endeavour he grew more successful as he grew older.

When the movement crystallized, Maurice, as Kingsley's adviser, gave him 'the highest proof of confidence' and recruited his help; and like Thomas Hughes, who was one of the first to join the founders, Kingsley was confident that they could set the world to rights in a trice. He went to work with a will:

> The day of the Lord is at hand, at hand:
>   Its storms roll up the sky;
> The nations sleep starving on heaps of gold;
>   All dreamers toss and sigh;
> The night is darkest before the morn;
> When the pain is sorest the child is born,
>   And the Day of the Lord at hand.
>
> Gather you, gather you, angels of God –
>   Freedom, and Mercy, and Truth;
> Come! for the earth is grown coward and old,
>   Come down, and renew her youth.
> Wisdom, Self-Sacrifice, Daring, and Love,
> Haste to the battle-field, stoop from above
>   To the Day of the Lord at hand.
>
> Gather you, gather you, hounds of hell –
>   Famine, and Plague, and War;
> Idleness, Bigotry, Cant, and Misrule,
>   Gather, and fall in the snare!
> Hireling and Mammonite, Bigot and Knave,
> Crawl to the battle-field, sneak to your grave,
>   In the Day of the Lord at hand.[9]

Reminiscent of Shelley's 'Mask of Anarchy', this forthright poem was included in Kingsley's sermon for Good Friday, 1850. He linked 'the day of the Lord' (Isaiah 58: 5–7) with 'the acceptable year of the Lord' (Luke IV: 16–21), and for him both passages implied renewal and redemption. During this period when Parson Lot felt most intensely, he 'seemed to look, with trembling, for the coming of great and terrible social convulsions, of a "day of the Lord", such as Isaiah [had] looked for, as the inevitable fate of a world grown evil, yet governed still by a righteous God'.[10] Both passages suggested the day on which Christian Socialism merged with the Chartism that it was soon to ameliorate and eventually to replace. And sensible of his mission as resembling Christ's at the beginning of His ministry, Kingsley chose 'the acceptable year of the

Lord' for the text of his *Message of the Church to Labouring Men* in June, 1851, which concluded his Parson Lot period.

He set the movement in motion on 12 April, 1848, by posting placards, which he had addressed to the Workmen of England, and signed, 'a Working Parson'. And however interpreted at the time, this day became a public act of atonement on the part of the Church for half a century of 'apostasy, of class-prejudice and political sycophancy'.[11] It also marked the beginning of a movement that cut across doctrinal and sectarian differences from the moment of its inception, and asserted once more the simple message of comfort and love that Christ had preached in His Sermon on the Mount.

The movement got properly under way with a penny periodical, *Politics for the People* (6 May–29 July, 1848), so that the public might know what the founders intended. On 22 April Maurice wrote a round of letters drumming up contributions for it. Thus to Archdeacon Hare, who had been his classical tutor at Cambridge and, at this point, besides his interest in the social question, was Maurice's brother-in-law:

My dear Julius,
I hope we are going on promisingly with the paper. The first article will be on 'Fraternity', explaining our principles and purposes, by me. There will be one on 'the People', on 'France under Louis Philippe', and on 'the Suffrage' (the first of a series), all by Ludlow; a sanitary article by Dr. Guy; I hope some verses from Kingsley. Could you bring us anything of any kind, long or short, original or translated?

And on the same day, to Kingsley:

I do hope the first number will go forth with God's blessing. We want poetry very much, and something on pictures (what you like), and could not you write ... about the right and wrong use of the Bible – I mean, protesting against the notion of turning it into a book for keeping the poor in order?[12]

Kingsley complied, and for the first number of *Politics* (6 May, 1848) produced anonymously the rollicking poem, 'The Working Man's Appeal':

No longer dream enchanted dreams,
    Nor moralize on flowers,
But nerve your hearts to worthier themes,
    And join your hands with ours.

. . .

Look forth beyond the labour-mart,
    Where Mammon want devours,
Confess a common human heart,
    And join your hands with ours!

And in response to Maurice's request for 'something on pictures', and using 'Parson Lot' for the first time, he supplied the first of three improving essays on the National Gallery. Since beauty was 'God's hand-writing', readers were urged never to lose an opportunity to feast upon it and picture galleries were recommended as 'the townsman's paradise of refreshment'.

In the second number of *Politics* he initiated his Letters to Chartists with this arresting opening:

I am a radical reformer. . . . My only quarrel with the charter is, that it does not go far enough in reform. I want to see you free. . . . It [the charter] disappointed me bitterly when I read it. . . . That French cry of 'Organization of Labour' is worth thousands of it, and yet that does not go to the bottom of the matter by many a mile.

Few read to the tame and orthodox climax of his argument:

God will only reform society on condition of our reforming every man his own self. . . . 'Be fit to be free, and God himself will set you free! Do God's work, and you will share God's wages. Trust in the Lord, and be doing good, dwell in the land, and verily, thou shalt be fed. Commit thy way unto the Lord, and He shall bring it to pass' (p. 28).

So rash a beginning naturally aroused alarm in brocaded Victorian drawing-rooms, and his reference to 'that French cry' was particularly disconcerting.

As one of the founders of the movement, Ludlow had proclaimed himself a follower of Louis Blanc (1811–62), whose teaching combined association with brotherly love along Guild Socialist lines. Although he was firmly convinced that socialism would destroy Christianity unless the Church 'christianized' it, and urged

Maurice, who shared his opinion, to accept the spiritual leadership of their movement, few people outside their immediate group knew this.

Louis Blanc had been a member of the provisional government set up after the revolution and was in exile in England as the Christian Socialists went to work. Bewailing the lack of freedom in France, he equated the growing liberalism in England with socialism, and from London issued the first number of his periodical, *The New World* (1849):

Among my friends, some are in prison, others banished in foreign lands. The cause to which I belong, has become for many mistaken minds, a subject of awe and scandal. The party I serve has lost, one by one, nearly all its leaders, most of its Journals have just been suppressed, and even its name is perhaps upon the point of being disputed. – In fine, at the moment I am writing, it is known by all, that for the second time since the Revolution of February, Paris is in a state of siege.[13]

With A. J. Scott's lectures on the development of socialism in France appearing in *Politics*,[14] and Ludlow's open approval of Louis Blanc, it was regrettable that Kingsley should also have appeared to condone French socialism. It was scarcely surprising that Englishmen feared revolutionary tendencies to be latent in Christian Socialism. Even though Maurice's first *Tract on Christian Socialism* had stated their principles very clearly, Kingsley, like many men at the time, had failed to realize that there was a world of difference between socialism and Christian socialism. Maurice had agreed with Owen, Fourier, and Louis Blanc to the extent that they all regarded co-operation as 'the social principle' and equally felt competition to be 'the dividing destructive principle' in society. But identifying Christianity with 'the older view of the Church', which he described as 'a fellowship constituted by God Himself in a divine and Human Person', he showed unmistakably how his 'Christian Socialism' belonged to the Church, and how it differed both from mere socialism and from communism.

For him, socialism was a matter of semantics. The word meant associating together in mutual co-operation. This was good as far as it went, and though excellent as a means to better relations between hands and heads, between labour and management, it did not go far enough. To be valid, socialism had to be Christianized, and Christian Socialism therefore meant associating together to form a society 'constituted in Christ'. Though a devout Christian, Ludlow seems not to have grasped this, and his failure to do so led to confusion among the members, including Kingsley, as we shall see in a moment. As for democracy, Maurice believed 'the voice of Demos' to be 'the devil's voice and not God's', largely because a majority (regardless of class) tended to clutch at power merely for the sake of power, and 'the tyranny of the majority' was the 'surest step' to the tyranny of a dictator.[15]

In his second Letter to Chartists Kingsley, acceding to Maurice's third request, spoke of the Bible as a handbook needed as much by the high as the low. Hell fire was not reserved for the humble alone, he argued. This letter was equally misguided, for it criticized the clergy for misusing the Bible as an instrument for coercing the poor, and although Kingsley had not excepted himself, it was not surprising that Hare complained to Maurice, declaring that the letter ought to have been suppressed.[16] Though the clergy had not fulfilled their duties, there were 'zealous and devoted men' among them, and Kingsley's letter had unfortunately fostered an opinion already much too prevalent among the Chartists, that the clergy were all 'cheating and juggling' them. The letter would do more harm than *Politics* could remedy in a twelvemonth, the Archdeacon thought.

Writings by Parson Lot continued to appear from time to time between May, 1848 and June, 1852.[17] *Politics* ceased on 29 July, 1848, but that month witnessed the first instalment of 'Yeast' in *Fraser's*. Kingsley wrote none of the *Tracts on Christian Socialism*, but of the *Tracts by Christian Socialists*, the second was a reprint of his *Cheap Clothes and Nasty*, an indignant Carlylean outburst exposing the 'sweating' system among the tailors and incidentally providing him with facts for *Alton Locke*. Parson Lot was also to contribute a series of 'Bible Politics' to *The Christian Socialist*, the official organ of the movement. All these publications helped to stimulate interest in social questions even if, at the same time, they annoyed, antagonized, and embarrassed, and even though, on occasion, they brought notoriety rather than fame to the writer. But they all had the merit of jolting the nation out of social indifference and Kingsley was already busy with literature of a higher order – *Yeast* and *Alton Locke*.

As the movement grew and others joined the group around Maurice, criticism intensified. The Reviews grew vitriolic, less because of social ideas in themselves than because of fears that conservative England should be heading in the direction of revolutionary republican France. Besieged from without, the group was soon dogged by differences from within. Ludlow wished association members to be avowed Christians, but Maurice opposed this on grounds of conscience. And because Ludlow felt that his views were 'diametrically opposite' to Maurice's, he was to give up the editorship of *The Christian Socialist* in 1852.[18] Their fundamental difference arose over the meaning of *socialism*.

Maurice had insisted that *democracy* and *socialism* were contraries, while Ludlow had identified democracy with 'People-government', and had declared it to be a necessary result of socialism. Lord Goderich (afterwards 1st Marquess of Ripon) was to adopt a similar view in his pamphlet, named *The Duty of the Age* by Kingsley and intended by him, Ludlow, and Lord Goderich to be the fifth *Tract by Christian Socialists*. The 'voice of Demos' and 'the tyranny of the majority' had risen again.

An avowed and open radical, Goderich nevertheless joined the Christian Socialists in the autumn of 1850, became a subscribing member of the Society for Promoting Working Men's Associations and joined its Central Board. 'A manly youth, good-hearted and merry, passionately devoted to shooting, fishing, and entomology', he made an ideal companion for Thomas Hughes and Kingsley, while his unbounded admiration for the *Associations Ouvrières* in France endeared him to Ludlow, who wished English associations to be modelled on their plan. *The Duty of the Age* made a strong plea for universal suffrage and self-government. It was 'the duty of the age' to abolish aristocracies, Goderich declared – himself, be it noted, 'a courtesy viscount and heir of two earldoms, a barony and a baronetcy'.[19] Appreciating his politics less than his popularity, Maurice suppressed the pamphlet, thus abruptly ending the *Tracts by Christian Socialists*.

Like Ludlow, Goderich had equated socialism and democracy,

whereas Maurice equated democracy and communism. Writing to Ludlow on 8 September, 1852, he was to emphasize that his concept of socialism meant an 'acknowledgement of brotherhood in heart and fellowship in work', and that this was 'the necessary fulfilment of the principle of the Gospel'.[20] However one might twist the word, democracy implied 'a right on the part of the people to choose, cashier, and depose their rulers', Maurice declared, and this was not Christ's way. People might govern themselves, but 'What I wish to know is, "*do they make* Christ their king?"'. Under Him, an earthly king is never above the law. On the contrary, the king stands as 'the witness for law from generation to generation', whereas when people govern themselves they tend as mere majorities to defend 'self-willed power'. The Gospel, Maurice had reminded Goderich, begins 'with the proclamation of an invisible and righteous King', and since earthly polity was to imitate the heavenly, the established order had to retain the elements of an organic Christian society comprising 'Monarchy, Aristocracy, and Socialism or rather Humanity'.

Bringing theology, politics, and history into one splendid unity, he also told Ludlow that history was to him 'the most beautiful unfolding of God's purpose for mankind, amidst all contradictions of human self-will'. He also emphasized in the same letter that both history and the genius of the English people recognized human inequalities and class differences as *given* and, therefore, as indispensable:

A king given, an aristocracy given, and I can see my way clearly to call upon them to do the work which God has laid upon them; ... But reconstitute society upon the democratic basis – treat the sovereign and the aristocracy as not intended to rule and guide the land, as only holding their commission from us – and I anticipate nothing but a most accursed sacerdotal rule or a military despotism, with the great body of the population in either case morally, politically, physically serfs, more than they are at present or ever have been.

That Kingsley understood and accepted Maurice's teaching is clear from his interpretation of his master in a sermon preached on 30 April, 1848, as part of the dedication ceremonies for a new church:

Men are crying out now a days for the People's Charter. I say, a new Church is the pledge of a Charter such as no Acts of Parliament can give, the pledge of liberty . . . the pledge of equality in the same Baptism, the same bread of life, the same Spirit of God – a pledge of fraternity and brotherhood . . . with every man and child who wears the human flesh and spirit which Christ our Saviour [wore]. This is the people's Charter – that they are members of the Kingdom of Christ.

But Kingsley loved a cause, and in his impetuosity he had grown aggressive and had allowed himself to be swept along on the stream of his enthusiasm as well as that of his personable and lordly friend. In 1848, the Christian socialists had initiated meetings with working-men. Though many of them were Chartists who had participated in the demonstration on the Tenth, Maurice was determined to hear their grievances in order that he and his group might the more readily help them. At one of these gatherings when 'the meeting waxed warm' and some of the men had begun attacking the Church, Kingsley, determined to preserve order as well as her good name, had arisen and declared – 'I am a Church of England parson' – a long pause – 'and a Chartist'.

Clergymen who met with working men and Chartists in 1848 were very brave, for they were defying custom and convention. But a clergyman who publicly declared himself a Chartist in 1848 was less brave than rash. Times being what they were, he could only be thought indiscreet. To his colleagues, his careless declaration emphasized his vehemence and sincerity. To those working men who actually believed him, it meant that he was deeply sympathetic with their cause. Though he had gone on to denounce their methods, his indiscretion had rendered him vulnerable to public attack and now, in an impulsive moment, he had sanctioned Goderich's pamphlet. But Maurice's suppression of it proved a salutary clarification for Kingsley the clergyman who was working with great intensity at his novels.

The Saint's Tragedy had brought Kingsley into the limelight early in 1848, and between this time and 1850 when *Alton Locke* appeared, his controversial tracts, letters, and other incunabula including *Cheap Clothes* had all appeared. His placards had asserted that the Charter, for which the Chartists had gravely threatened the peace of London but two days earlier, did not go 'far enough' in reform; and most readers, put off at once, had failed to read his statement in the same placard that, in his view, the Chartist's were 'trying to do God's work with the devil's tools'. Archdeacon Hare's strictures on his unfortunate Letters to Chartists have already been mentioned, as well as the general disapproval attending Kingsley's recommendation of the Bible as a guide for radical reformers. Attacking the squirearchy, 'Yeast' had reduced the circulation of *Fraser's*, and was therefore cut short with the sixth instalment. *Cheap Clothes* had embarrassed and had roused feelings of public guilt, which *Alton Locke* had intensified; and the publication of *Yeast* in book form in 1851 seemed a further affront. All these turbulent and ill-digested publications, pelting down suddenly like hail on a hot summer's day had set Kingsley's world reeling in amazement, and neither his anonymity nor his pseudonym could save him from the harsh and equally ill-digested reprisals that followed on the heels of the storm he had raised. The author of them was quickly identified with the preacher, and both with Charles Kingsley who, as we shall see, reflected himself in his novels.

Thriving on the very division it fostered, the periodical press leapt into action. The *Guardian* attacked *Yeast* on 7 May, 1851, and in his refutation on 14 June, Maurice revealed Kingsley's identity so that there was no excuse for the Rev. G. S. Drew's attack on Kingsley's sermon preached in Drew's church on 22 June. Then, in September, the *Quarterly Review* published a long and scathing article entitled 'Revolutionary Literature'.[21] It declared *Alton Locke* to be a defence of 'Chartist socialism' and an 'unEnglish menace' leading to bloody revolution. Adopting a similar view, the *Edinburgh Review* had followed with a bitter attack, not only on *Alton Locke* but on *Cheap Clothes*, and on Maurice's first *Tract* as well. It had utterly ignored the vital epithet 'Christian'.[22] On 18 October, barely two months after the book had come out in 1850, *The Times* had devoted three-and-one-half columns to a review of *Alton Locke* under the heading, 'The Autobiography of a Chartist', and had warned its readers to 'beware of confounding the shortcomings of a nation's governors with the faults and crimes of the governed'. They thus struck the key-note of the more justifiable criticism, but they too had failed to see that the work was actually propounding Christian socialism.

Among the novels, only *Yeast* and *Alton Locke* are overtly Christian Socialist propaganda, although *Two Years Ago* dealing with sanitation as it does, may be included in this category as well. The novels, however, rise to the spiritual level expected of a clergyman possessed of Maurice's ideas, and they are all superior to these initial writings. But all of Kingsley's novels, whether contemporaneous problem pieces or historical period pastiches, uphold Christian principles and practices as vital for the well-being of the nation, and in this sense Kingsley's novels are all apologies for Christian socialism.

Kingsley's early work has been stressed in order to show the degree to which he was committed to the regeneration of society. Christian socialism had come into the arena of nineteenth-century thought to assist in the struggle between Benthamite *laissez-faire* and Coleridgean transcendentalism and, although the practical activity diminished in vigour during 1853 and ceased altogether on 23 November, 1854, for Maurice and Kingsley the movement was religious and philosophical, and was therefore an integral part of the liberal Christianity which they continued to inculcate throughout their respective careers as clergymen in the English church. The mission of both men was to Christianize the socialism then coming into the country by socializing the exclusive doctrinal Christianity that characterized the period, and the novels were increasingly to emphasize both individual and national regeneration.

When Kingsley rose to preach *The Message of the Church to Labouring Men* in 1851, he was thus already a well-known man, and his sermons only served to fix him in the public mind as a preacher whose power in the pulpit corroborated the power of his pen. The Rev. G. S. Drew of St. John's, Fitzroy Square, had invited him to preach to the working men in London for the Great Exhibition, and Kingsley had accepted the invitation through Maurice. The sermon not only summarized, but climaxed the confusing and often painful conflicts that had attended the movement. Ultimately, too, it placed Kingsley's approach to reform on the Christian foundation promulgated by Maurice, vindicated Kingsley's own orthodoxy in the Church, and brought about the demise of Parson Lot as well as banishing Kingsley's anonymity. It also clarified the nature of his literary purposes and paved the way for a more tolerant attitude to his later novels. For this study, the sermon rounds out the sketch of the author's activities between 1848 and 1851, completing that phase of his career which projected his novels.

The text of the sermon was the same as that which had filled the minds of the founders on 10 April, and which was central to much of Kingsley's thinking during the decade of the novels. But it was especially meaningful, as we have seen, during this, his Parson Lot period. Announcing his text, he summed up 'the acceptable year of the Lord' in three words – freedom, equality, and brotherhood; and his exposition of them turned on the axiom that every great truth comes forth with an attendant counterfeit. Thus there are two kinds of liberty – the false, when a man does as he likes; and the true, when he does as he ought. Of equality there are two kinds also – the false, which reduces intellects and characters to a dead level, 'ending in the grossest kind of inequality'; and the true, the spiritual equality, proclaimed by the Church wherein each man, though individual in character and faculties, has an equal opportunity 'to educate and to use his talents' according to his ability, and to be rewarded proportionally. And there are two kinds of brotherhood – the false, which chooses friends exclusively; and the true, which finds all men brothers in Christ.

The third part of his sermon presented the message of the Church which bore witness '*for* God's kingdom on earth', and whose sacraments symbolized the different aspects of that kingdom: the Bible announced man's freedom; Baptism, his equality; and the Holy Communion, his brotherhood. In the light of what we have said of Maurice's theology in Chapter 1, this is now familiar matter. It was also pronounced orthodox by the Bishop of London but, alas, belatedly.

The effect of this message on Kingsley's audience was electric. Accustomed as they were to the well-turned and intoned phraseology typical of the nineteenth-century parson in the pulpit, Kingsley's hearers were struck by the direct and forthright statements set forth in language, logical, simple, and emotionally appealing. Secondly, as Kingsley announced his text, the 'Spirit of the Lord' that was upon Jesus when He had risen to preach 'the acceptable year of the Lord' was, by analogy, upon Kingsley, and was felt by the nature of his utterance to be upon him. Again, the plain and simple words, as Kingsley expounded the text, made the Trinitarian foundation of the kingdom, implicit in the text, startlingly obvious.

But, finally, it was Kingsley's words about the business of 'a Christian priest in a Christian nation' that jolted his congregation:

I assert that the business for which God sends a Christian priest into a Christian nation is, to preach freedom, equality, and brotherhood, in the fullest, deepest, widest meaning of those three great words; that in as far as he does, he is a true priest, doing his Lord's work with his Lord's blessing on him; that in as far as he does not he is no priest at all, but a traitor to God and man.

More than that, as all 'his strength, physical, mental, and moral' found expression in his keen grey eyes, which fixed his congregation with the gaze of an eagle, Kingsley woke them to a sense of crisis such as they had not felt before, as he asserted that 'if the traitorous priest persevered in his mistake . . . about his own work', retribution would surely come:

. . . the Lord of that priest will come in an hour when he is not aware, and in a way that he thinketh not of, and will, in fearful literalness cut him asunder! and appoint him his portion with the unbelievers, where will be weeping and gnashing of teeth. I assert this in solemn earnest.

The sermon ended, he was about to pronounce the blessing when up rose Rev. G. S. Drew, who declared that much of the sermon was both 'dangerous' and 'untrue'.[23] Amidst the doctrinal discord of the age, it was the message of the Christian Church heard but too rarely, and it shows the extent to which Kingsley was able to interpret Maurice, to whom, to repeat Kingsley's own declaration, he owed 'the foundation' of a 'coherent view of the word of God, and the meaning of the Church of England'. Excitement rippled through the congregation, but Kingsley quietly withdrew to the vestry, thus narrowly averting an unseemly uproar.

It was not the content of the sermon, but the trenchant and direct language in which it was cast that had frightened the clergyman; and it was the same powerful language that in *Yeast* and *Alton Locke* had roused the public and the press. No other response could more forcibly have expressed the impact of the sermon, which tellingly illustrated Kingsley's 'power of cutting out what he meant in a few clear words'. The priest and the poet had united in him to direct that power to the more literary purposes of Christian teaching. It was substantially the same language that was to make *Hypatia*, *Westward Ho!*, and *Hereward the Wake* the great memorials to Maurice that they are, and the same that has given Kingsley his unique place in English literature. In the novels, the words of his sermons are made flesh.

Increasingly Kingsley had come to see a moral relationship between nature and human suffering. Back in Eversley, troubled more by the possible effect of the incident on the workmen, who had witnessed the scene, than pained by the unwarranted insult he had received, the poet-priest recalled an incident from a boyhood experience, the tragic shipwreck off the coast of Clovelly, which had juxtaposed nature and human nature. The vividness with which in *Prose Idylls* he recalls the break-up of the ship reveals at once the strength of his imagination and the force of the moral lesson it had taught him.

As the black mass of the ship pitched and strained, she seemed 'vainly to implore the help of man against the stern ministers of the Omnipotent'. To Charles and his brothers, who had watched with the group of agonized villagers on the shore, she assumed the 'horrible image' of a human being 'shrieking upon the rack', and her death struggle had taught him the great travail in nature herself:

We turned at last away; when lo! a wave, huger than all before it, rushed up the boulders towards us. – We had just time to save ourselves. – A dull, thunderous groan, as if a mountain had collapsed, rose above the roar of the tempest; and we all turned with an instinctive knowledge of what had happened, just in time to see the huge mass melt away into the boiling white, and vanish for ever more. And then the very raving of the wind seemed hushed with awe; the very breakers plunged more silently towards the shore, with something of a sullen compunction.[24]

The same conflict raged in the hearts of men as they looked upon that usually 'merry beach beside the town', now 'covered with shrieking women . . . as corpse after corpse swept up at the feet of wife and child'. The whole town sorrowed for those who had gone out the night before 'in the fulness of strength and courage'. Recalling the anguished fisher-folk and their conflict, so like his own in his hour of trial, he wrote,

> But men must work, and women must weep
> Though storms be sudden, and waters deep,
> And the harbour bar be moaning.

Poetic expression had given him relief.

But the storm was not over. The morning papers had branded him a radical and an apostle of socialism; and Dr. Blomfield, the Bishop of London, had forbidden him to preach in his diocese. On the other hand, extreme Chartists and dissenters, believing Kingsley to be at one with them, offered him the use of their lecture-hall, declaring their allegiance and co-operation. How little the people had understood.

The sermon, printed in the form in which it had been preached, and introduced by Maurice, was circulated to vindicate Kingsley; and having read it, the Bishop revoked his edict. The sermon was orthodox after all. But Kingsley knew no pleasure. Worn with the controversies of the time and utterly exhausted, he nevertheless turned to his task,

> For men must work, and women must weep,
> And the sooner it's over, the sooner to sleep;
> And good-bye to the bar and its moaning.

Born of the experience, 'The Three Fishers' had enabled him to transcend it.

As he had overcome the attack on the *Message of the Church*, so must he now rise above contemporary muddlement. At Maurice's request he had published his political creed in the *Christian Socialist* (14 December, 1850) and there he had begged leave to state that he believed the King of kings to be 'the fountain of all authority', and that the Queen and all her magistrates were 'His minister'. While he also approved of extending the franchise he felt that it should be done cautiously, and only after due preparation. He also declared the 'modern French dogma, that the will of the people is the source of power', to be 'atheistic in theory and impossible in practice'. His mentor, after all, had shown *socialism* and *democracy* to be opposing policies of social organization, while *Christian socialism* was an association of human beings under God, a 'fellowship' of rich and poor, high and low, constituted in Christ,[25] and Kingsley was to turn this to account with ever-growing facility as he proceeded from novel to novel.

Parson Lot had finished his work when he had roused the nation. But one whose writings stirred people up so effectively had great power, and Kingsley had already demonstrated the nature of that power on two levels. On the eve of their movement he had published *The Saint's Tragedy*, a theological blank-verse drama on the theme of self-sacrifice. While the play was perhaps 'a little too bold for the taste and temper of the age', Maurice, who wrote the preface for it, none the less recognized the incisive diction and the sinewy strength of the language, and he was greatly impressed with the degree to which his disciple's thought corresponded with his own. Kingsley had also produced controversial and polemical work in language so compelling that men were driven to act. Maurice saw that his very sensitive and gifted disciple wrote and spoke intensely because of his profound conviction that Christian association had ultimately to be accepted by the human race 'if it would save its soul alive', and he was ready to pardon Parson Lot's sayings and doings for the promise they manifested. Under his guidance, Kingsley was already reading for *Hypatia*, but we must now turn to *Yeast* and *Alton Locke*.

CHAPTER 3

Yeast

'These papers', wrote Kingsley of *Yeast*,[1] 'have been, from beginning to end, as in name, so in nature, Yeast – an honest sample of the questions which . . . are rapidly leavening the minds of the rising generation'. An unusually appropriate title for the novel, it may have derived from John Keats, whose work was revived in 1848 by Monckton Milnes. Keats had seen in the best of men 'a kind of spiritual yeast' which created 'the ferment' of their existence, and which 'propell'd' them 'to act and strive and buffet with Circumstance'.[2] This was the kind of yeast that Kingsley desired for his generation and, like Keats, he knew that it had to come from within. The yeast of which he speaks is spiritual regeneration, and this is the theme of the book.

Determined that no one should miss the point, he inserted a *nota bene* expletive between the title and the chapter-head of the first instalment in *Fraser's Magazine*.[3] Reciprocity between himself and his readers, he said, depended 'mainly on the sort of soil' into which his story should fall in 'the brain-gardens of a reading public', and he therefore asked his readers to 'believe' that the narrative had 'a spiritual sequence', which those who read with imaginative faith would see in the 'fruits' it bore.

Evidently placed by design at the core of *Yeast*, the promised 'sequence' is none other than Paul Tregarva's short account of his conversion on a night many years before, when he was sixteen. The 'ghastly ha! ha! ha!' of a stone-plover suddenly reminds him of the first time he had heard that bird, and since it was associated in his memory with his conversion, the cry recalls his experience. As Squire Lavington's gamekeeper, he tells his story to Lancelot Smith, the hero, who accompanied him to a sordid revel in order to observe the social vapidity of the villagers:

It was a wild, whirling grey night, with the air full of sleet and rain [he began]. . . . I lost my way across the moors. . . . They were burrowed like a rabbit-warren with old mine-shafts. . . . I got into a great furze-croft, full of deads (those are the earth-heaps they throw out of the shafts), where no man in his senses dare go forward or back in the dark, for fear of the shafts; and the wind and the snow were so sharp, they made me quite stupid and sleepy; and I knew if I stayed there I should be frozen to death, and if I went on, there were the shafts ready to swallow me up: and what with fear and the howling and raging of the wind, I was like a mazed boy . . . (Ch. XIII, 216).

The eerie setting renders the experience that follows the more plausible. But although Tregarva had spoken of his conversion as 'turning to one whom he had known all along, and disregarded', Lancelot had failed to grasp its significance. Yet the ferment in his mind had made him interested in the gamekeeper's story:

I was down on my knees among the furze-bushes, and I tried to pray; but I was too frightened, for I felt the beast I had been, sir; and I expected the ground to open and let me down every moment; and then there came over my head a rushing, and a cry. 'Ha! ha! ha! Paul!' it said; and it seemed as if all the devils and witches were out on the wind, a-laughing at my misery. 'Oh, I'll mend – I'll repent', I said, 'indeed I will': and again it came back, – 'Ha! ha! ha! Paul!' it said. I knew afterwards that it was a bird; but the Lord sent it to me for a messenger, no less, that night. And I shook like a reed in the water; and then, all at once a thought struck me. 'Why should I be a coward? Why should I be afraid of shafts, or devils, or hell, or anything else? If I am a miserable sinner, there's One died for me – I owe Him love, not fear at all. I'll not be frightened into doing right – that's a rascally reason for repentance.' And so it was, sir, that I rose up like a man, and said to the Lord Jesus, right out into the black, dumb air, – 'If you'll be on my side this night, good Lord, that died for me, I'll be on your side for ever, villain as I am, if I'm worth making any use of'. And there and then, sir, I saw a light come over the bushes, brighter, and brighter, up to me; and there rose up a voice within me, and spoke to me, quite soft and sweet, – 'Fear not, Paul, for I will send thee far hence unto the Gentiles'. And what more happened I can't tell, for when I woke I was safe at home (Ch. XIII, 218).

This tale parallels the Biblical accounts of conversion already outlined in Chapter 1. St. Paul hears the call, 'Saul, Saul, why persecutest thou me?', and at once he asks, 'What wilt thou have me do?'. Unlike the converts of the Old Testament, Paul experiences a period of darkness and one naturally attaches significance to the first words of Ananias, who addresses him as 'brother'. Upon the pronouncement of brotherhood Paul sees the light. He is baptized, and at once begins preaching the kingdom.[4]

Kingsley depicts Paul Tregarva as a second Saul, a second Paul. Like the saint's, Paul's experience begins, not with a total vision, but with an awareness of supernatural forces at work upon him. The process is initiated with 'a rushing and a cry'. The 'ha! ha! ha! Paul!' is a clarion call arousing his conscience to a prevision of what is to come. Then follows darkness accompanied by feelings of inadequacy and doubt. In due course, self-abasement brings a determination to atone, and this feeling is expressed in the pent-up cry, 'Oh, I'll mend – I'll repent, indeed I will', after which there flows in upon him the certainty of absolution fraught with comfort and peace. 'Why should I be a coward?' asks Paul. 'If I'm a miserable sinner, there's One died for me – I owe Him love, not fear at all'. With the promise to 'be on His side for ever', the vision breaks upon him as 'a light [comes] over the bushes, brighter and brighter'. Lastly, as in the Biblical prototype, the vision enables him to hear the 'voice within', the call to labour, with its implied promise of supernatural help: 'Fear not, Paul, for I will send thee far hence unto the Gentiles'.

All this is rendered credible by commonplace reality: the cry of the bird, the approaching lanterns, and the 'dead faint' in which Paul is found. Yet the experience is graven for ever on his mind and, as a converted man a sense of mission possesses him, which henceforth directs his life. He is now a man who believes in God. His day-star had risen and his voice, strangely that also of God, now guides Lancelot Smith to his change of heart. Paul's mission has taken him out of himself to the assistance of those around him, and thus we see Christian socialism in action. This is the 'spiritual sequence' that Kingsley asked his readers to find in *Yeast*.

But Kingsley carried this capsulated account further. Since the steps in Paul Tregarva's conversion provided him with a sequence for the whole novel, he used it both narratively and structurally. In other words, Paul's account, re-applied, expanded, and adapted, becomes the hero's story and Lancelot's change, in turn, is interwoven with the heroine's tale. Paul Tregarva's account of his regenerative experience lies in the heart of the book, while the more prolonged experiences of Lancelot, Argemone, and others unfold round it like petals opening round the heart of a rose as each convert responds to the charity, co-operation, and hope that nurture spiritual renewal in the community. The double but complementary conversions of Lancelot and Argemone represent the novel's action and, like yeast in rising dough, the processes introduce changes and thus resolve the many problems 'leavening the minds of the rising generation'.

The hero's story is quickly told. Lancelot Smith is a wealthy young man who has never thought of anything but fun and fine clothes. As the story begins, he is discontented and confused, but because he has been reading Francis de Sales' *Introduction to a Devout Life*, his conscience is astir. He sees a 'ghastly discord' in the fox-hunt in which he is engaged and, somehow, the whole world seems out of joint. Reigning his horse to ruminate, he is startled by the sudden appearance of Argemone Lavington, and for one brief moment Lancelot and Argemone meet face to face and fall utterly in love: each displaces the self with the other, a welcome stranger. Equally suddenly, Lancelot's vicious mount gallops off, throwing him from the saddle. He suffers a brain concussion and is plunged into darkness. He makes a slow recovery at Whitford Priors, the home of Squire Lavington, and as he does so he emerges from the 'blackness of night' into a new day. His 'new feeling' for Argemone returns with that day, and leads him to conclude that the world, once so sadly out of joint, is now 'wonderful', and the human race positively 'glorified'.

Meanwhile, he is not allowed to lose himself in his own happiness, and is tested by sore trials. Mrs. Lavington disapproves of his interest in Argemone, largely because he has no vocation in life and seems disinclined to find one. Then, a blow strikes his family. They lose their fortune and Lancelot, suddenly without a penny, is forced to find work. While this seeming ill luck places him outside of Argemone's world, it has unrecognized advantages in teaching him patience, sympathy with the poor and, above all, the joy of helping others. Three characters assist him in changing his outlook on life. Paul Tregarva, as we have seen, shows him the meaning of conversion and, with that, the shocking state of contemporary society.

Argemone Lavington, who has been caring for the poor on her father's estate, shows him the true meaning of work and, at the close of the novel, Barnakill, the prophet, completes their teaching by directing him into practical action.

Paul Tregarva teaches his pupil that contemporary society is sadly insouciant to the poor. Their present world, Paul contends, drives men to seek wealth for themselves rather than their country and, this being so in his view, the race resembles 'a herd of cowardly wild cattle': though they may feed together, in accord with their natures they invariably leave the sick and helpless among them to perish. This attitude, prevalent in nineteenth-century society, is animal rather than human, and utterly opposes the 'true society' denoted variously in the Bible as a 'living tree', a 'holy brotherhood', and a 'kingdom of God'. Quite clearly, Paul reminds Lancelot, England has forgotten God and is following a spurious 'christianity' that must be replaced with the practical teaching of Jesus Christ (Ch. VIII, 115).

For her part, Argemone convinces Lancelot of the necessity for national atonement, and this is not unconnected with history. Her own home, Whitford Priors, had been the convent of the Whitford nuns, and there is a superstition in the community that the place is under a curse pronounced upon the Commissioners of Henry VIII by the Prioress herself when they imputed impurity to her and confiscated her convent. She is reputed to have ended her life in grief and distraction in the weir pool, since known as the Nun-pool, and not until the weir is dismantled and the cleansing waters allowed once more to wash the neglected villages below can the curse be removed. Though Argemone is not superstitious she is, like the nuns of old time, deeply devout, and her preoccupation with the poor puzzles Lancelot, but his own loss of fortune alters his thinking. Through her untiring efforts on their behalf she teaches him that national atonement for the sins of the past begins on a personal level.

Cogitating on these matters and sensing the change taking place in him, Lancelot queries Paul about the effect of his conversion on him: 'Did any real, practical change in your behaviour take place after that night?', he asks the gamekeeper when he has finished his

story. Paul's reply is something of a revelation to the ruminating
Lancelot:

As much, sir, as if you had put a soul into a hog, and told him that he was a
gentleman's son; and, if every time he remembered that, he got spirit
enough to conquer his hoggishness, and behave like a man, till the
hoggishness died out of him, and the manliness grew up and bore fruit
in him, more and more each day (Ch. XIII, 219).

Manliness requires courage, and Paul has shown rectitude on
behalf of the poor. Dismissed from Squire Lavington's service for
'A Rough Rhyme on a Rough Matter', a poem attacking the
indifference of the squirearchy to their tenant-workers, Paul
regards his misfortune with equanimity:

'I am a tall man', he said, 'like Saul the son of Kish; and I am going forth'
like him, sir, to find my father's asses. I doubt I shan't have to look far for
some of them'.
'And perhaps', said Lancelot laughing, 'to find a kingdom'.
'May be so, sir. I have found one already, by God's grace, and I'm much
mistaken if I don't begin to see my way towards another'.
'And what is that?'
'The kingdom of God on earth, sir, as well as in heaven. Come it must,
sir, and come it will some day'.
Lancelot shook his head.
Tregarva lifted up his eyes and said, – 'Are we not taught to pray for the
coming of His kingdom, sir?' . . . Lancelot was silent. The words gained a
new and blessed meaning in his eyes (Ch. XI, 178).

Between them, Argemone and Paul transform Lancelot. Paul
opts for a 'kingdom of God on earth' while Argemone, by nursing
the fever-patients, is already doing what she can to make that
kingdom a reality also; but through her devotion she succumbs
to the fever herself. The meaning of her selflessness dawns upon
Lancelot, and in response to Paul's living example and her dying
wish he promises to carry on her work. One of the most sordid
villages on the Whitford Priory estate, Ashy must be 'baptised'.
He, Lancelot, must dismantle the weir and free the Nun-pool,
thus sweeping away the pestilence and transforming Ashy into a
beautiful place 'among great flower-gardens' where children may
frolic and sing. The development of God's kingdom in this festering,
fever-ridden village is clearly his duty, and that must be his mission.

His fortune lost, his loved one dead, and possessed of nothing but the firm conviction that the contemporary credit system is a 'selfish counterfeit of God's order of love and trust', Lancelot determines to earn his living by following their examples, but it is hard for one who has never worked. Barnakill the prophet assists him in initiating his mission:

'Do you want work?' [asks that mysterious personage].
'Yes, if you have any'.
'Follow me, and carry a trunk from a shop to my lodgings.' . . . Lancelot set the trunk inside the door.
'What do you charge?'
'Sixpence'.
Barnakill looked him steadily in the face, gave him the sixpence, went in, and shut the door (Ch. XVII, 288).

Lancelot has triumphantly translated his 'new feeling' into action, and has thus begun his mission of service to others.

The conversional pattern is easily recognized in this brief sketch, and Argemone Lavington's conversion follows a pattern similar to Lancelot's. As the novel begins she too is shut up in the prison of self until her conscience stirs in response to his when he gives her a pen-and-ink drawing, entitled *The Triumph of Woman*. In the foreground is a desert broken only by occasional glimpses of a 'wandering watercourse', and in it are scattered groups 'in the dress and insignia of every period and occupation'. Kingsley describes the central figure:

Down the path of the morning beams, came Woman, clothed only in the armour of her own loveliness. Her bearing was stately, and yet modest; in her face pensive tenderness seemed wedded with earnest joy. In her right hand lay a cross, the emblem of self-sacrifice.

Power is manifested less in Woman herself than in the 'human tenderness and intelligence' which she lights up in the face of each man:

The scholar dropt his book, the miser his gold, the savage his weapons; even in the visage of the half-slumbering sot some nobler recollection seemed wistfully to struggle into life.

Not only does she inspire these, but the musician and the poet are also hypnotized and even the philosopher, who has suffered 'all the sorrows of his race', sees her as a 'preacher more mighty than himself'.

Urging his approbation of woman, Kingsley depicts a youth as the one in the sketch most deeply affected; and in spite of his fantastic dress, he is seen to resemble Lancelot Smith:

A youth . . . stood with clasped hands and brimming eyes, as remorse and pleasure struggled in his face; and as he looked, the fierce sensual features seemed to melt, and his flesh came again to him like the flesh of a little child (Ch. x, 149–50).

Esteemed a mightier preacher than the poet, Woman has touched his heart and, like Shelley in his *Hymn to Intellectual Beauty*, the young Lancelot experiences a transformation. Argemone sees that the central figure resembles herself, and suddenly grasps the lesson the sketch was meant to teach: she is the 'lodestar of all their emotions' and she, above all, is the lodestar of Lancelot Smith. Since 'love is like a flame' which grows by dispersion, she and Lancelot may light flame after flame in regenerating society, and the vision of a 'new destiny' breaks upon her. Her social conscience awake, she discards tractarianism and intellectual pride in doctrinal analysis, and thus begins a new life.

Love grows and bears fruit. Just as she has found in Lancelot one whose regeneration she can devotedly effect, so now she uses her new spirit in the interests of her neighbours. In obedience to her unseeing parents, she sublimates her love for him in disinterested service, making her mission an act of repentance for the Lavington family in servicing their own poor; and, as we have seen, she commits her work to Lancelot when she can no longer carry on the task.

When next the lovers meet, Argemone is on her death-bed. She tells him how 'the curse of the Lavington's has come upon her', how she must die for the people whom they, the wealthy Lavington's have made. She tells him

how she had gone up to the fever patients at Ashy. . . . She hinted at the horrible filth and misery she had seen, at the foul scents which had sickened her. A madness of remorse, she said, had seized her. She had

gone, in spite of her disgust, to several houses which she found open.
There were worse cottages . . . than even her own father's (Ch. XVI, 281).

In the spirit of Christ, that also of the ancient nuns of Whitford,
she helps the poor thus cancelling the curse:

The Nunpool! Take all the water, every drop, and wash Ashy clean again!
Make a great fountain in it – beautiful marble – to bubble and gurgle,
and trickle and foam, for ever and ever, and wash away the sins of the
Lavington's (Ch. XVI, 282).

Symbolizing baptism, this passage also indicates the regenerative
influence of sanitation in practical life but structurally, it unites
Lancelot's story with Argemone's, and both with the pattern
outlined by Paul Tregarva.

In Barnakill unite the mutual influences of Argemone Lavington
and Lancelot Smith. The prophet imparts the full significance of
the kingdom, first, in terms of human relationships, then, in terms
of the Spirit at work in those relationships. As the Spirit had risen
up and given life to the dry bones in the Valley of Vision, so now it
infuses and enlivens the body of nineteenth-century England.
Lancelot envisions the new Church: as Barnakill leads him through
the great west door of St. Paul's cathedral, he thinks neither of that
fabric of 'petrified religion', nor of the pall of commercial life
around it, but of Jesus Christ, the Man. An ideal upon whom men
have built an image of the City of God, He is the foundation of
the Church, and every man who emulates Him is part of that
Church. Every man who emulates Him also serves others in love
and self-sacrifice in the creation of that Church, the New Society.

With one convert playing a central role, and the conversions
of the two principal characters unfolding in its pages, *Yeast*, then, is
a study in conversion.[5] But the sequence that Kingsley had asked his
readers to note is obscured for a number of reasons. He had
introduced many problems that clouded the issue, and the *nota bene*
expletive was dropped from the novel itself. Without conscious
attention to the didactic bent of the book, readers mistook the
sequential changes in the unfolding characterizations for negative
rather than positive qualities, for they involved the old paradox
of losing one's life to find it.

EDINBURGH UNIVERSITY LIBRARY
CANCELLED

In the revelation of character, a gradual growth in the selflessness – in mystical terms, in the 'unselfing' – of the hero is disconcerting in terms of sequence, and the double conversions of Argemone and Lancelot only double the seeming anomaly. Nor was it easy, without an awareness focused on Kingsley's directive, for the average reader to see, even after the concise account of Paul Tregarva's conversion in the heart of the half-told tale of the principals, that Lancelot's more slowly unfolding sequence was in fact an extension surrounding Paul's. Once it is seen that Lancelot and Argemone are moving independently from a world of self-contained unreality to one of genuine reality, with whose regeneration each is concerned, there is no problem. Even the *Guardian* reviewer had not missed the theme of conversion, since he comments that 'the doctrine' in the book can 'convert' no one. But he inadvertently admits the contrary since, as each character turns to God, so *Yeast* turns the thoughts of readers to His fatherly government, and the novel becomes a delineation of the systolic aspect of conversion, as his use of the word suggests.

Yeast includes a counterfeit conversion. In expanding his serial Kingsley wove the tale of Lancelot's Tractarian cousin, Luke, into the novel (Chs. V, VIII, XII, XV). Buffeted by every kind of religious controversy with which the age was plagued, Luke had grown to feel that the Church of Rome was his sure and certain refuge. She would subdue his animal spirit; she would be the keeper of his conscience; and, with the aid of purgatory, she would guarantee his salvation. A foil for the regenerative process already discussed, Luke's 'conversion' represents a change from one religious system to another.

In the exchange of letters between Lancelot and his cousin other systems are also mentioned. Quakerism and Calvinism are included with Tractarianism, and money-making is suggested as the only pursuit permitted by Puritanism. Preaching the kingdom of Christ as 'divinely founded' by the King of kings, Maurice and Kingsley, as we remind ourselves, found all systems equally spurious. The Roman church was especially anathema precisely because her system, hardened by centuries of human obfuscation had, by her own claim, grown infallible, and thus excelled all other systems in the power of her appeal. But in *Yeast*, Luke turns from Tractarianism to Romanism in 'selfish superstitious terror' for the salvation of his own soul. He is as self-seeking for spiritual, as is his 'veteran Mammonite' father, the banker, for material gains. His mission, to the extent that he has one, is centred in himself.

The supreme task of every genuine convert, however, is the conversion of the world through an unbroken succession of individual conversions. As Kingsley put it, 'a great truth received into the depths of the soul germinates there and bears fruit a thousandfold'. The England of 1848 was in a state of perversion and, as a converted clergyman, Kingsley had envisaged the ultimate re-conversion of England. This was the kind of vision that had caught up his imagination as he turned to the popularization of Maurice's theology. He saw no conflict in his task: the Church and the Christian Socialist Movement both aimed at the regeneration of the nation, and thus of the Church herself. Nor can we over-emphasize the importance of the theme in nineteenth-century literature, and we may compare Kingsley's treatment of it with that of John Henry (afterwards Cardinal) Newman (1801–90), and with that of James Anthony Froude (1818–94), historian and brother of Richard Hurrell Froude, the intimate friend and follower of Newman, and a leader in the Oxford Movement, which Anthony renounced. It may also be noted that Anthony became Kingsley's brother-in-law.

To the extent that *Loss and Gain* (1848) and *The Nemesis of Faith* (1849) are autobiographical, Newman and Froude each show a sense of mission very different from that of Kingsley. Charles Reding, Newman's leading character, forsakes the English church for that of Rome, like Newman himself. Again like his creator, Reding is slowly convinced that his personal salvation is secure in the infallible system of the Roman dispensation, while for that of society at large he has little concern. In *The Nemesis*, on the other hand, Markham Sutherland, though deeply troubled by the con-temporary social situation, nevertheless, like Froude himself, succumbs to scepticism. While believing in the divine Founder and His teaching, he declares the Reformation to have 'cut the roots' of historical Christianity and thus to have deprived it of

Christ's love. He never gets beyond the first, or doubting phase of the conversion sequence, and never achieves a sense of mission, which is the final stage of that experience.

Though *Loss and Gain* lacks the glow of Kingsley's vision, it is, like *Yeast*, a systole: it promulgates conversion. To the extent, however, that *The Nemesis* is a conversion piece, it offers no such comfort. Like *Alton Locke* without its final chapters, it is a diastolic delineation of a nation of hollow men, portraying inhabitants of a land already desolate. The England of 1848 *is* in a state of 'perversion': but for Newman and Kingsley redemption is always possible, while for Froude it is not. They may be said to begin where he appears to end.

Froude, who turned from Newman and the Oxford Movement, adopted an independent position. Like Carlyle whose disciple he became, he 'raises questions he cannot answer'. However, he squarely faces the nineteenth-century issue, that of belief tempering a way of life. 'Was England Catholic, or was she Protestant?' He also clarifies the fundamental difference between the two disciplines: Catholicism, he said, depresses and subdues the 'external character of man', whereas Protestantism cultivates man 'outwards on every side', and insists on 'self-reliance'. Contemporary England, 'the strongest', is clearly 'the most Protestant' country in the world.

As Froude saw the Oxford Movement, Newman wished to infuse England's worldly Church with so much of the 'old life' as should enable her to do at home the 'same work' as the Roman Church was doing abroad. Froude insisted, however, that such an infusion would 'substitute devotion, endurance, humility, self-denial, sanctity, and faith' for things vital to Protestants – 'poetry, courage, daring, enterprise, resolution, and broad honest understanding': England would 'cease the produce great men'.

Kingsley and the Christian socialists, like Englishmen generally, had no wish to 'unprotestantize' England. Their re-conversion, while broadly catholic, excluded the possibility of a return to the medieval social system. Like Newman, Kingsley wished to see greater devotion, endurance, and humility among Englishmen, more self-denial, sanctity, and faith. But these qualities were not to be achieved at the expense of poetry, courage, daring, enterprise, resolution, and broad honest understanding. A great nation is articulate, and if her literary voice grows weak her understanding, resolution, enterprise, daring, and courage also grow weak and rapidly decline.

Frequently more evangelical than Maurice, Kingsley was vehemently in favour of the Reformation. 'Protestantism', he wrote in *Yeast*, 'is the cause of England and Christianity, and civilization, and freedom, and common sense'. For him, sanctity implied unmanliness and this, in turn, suggested a renunciation of nature. He insisted that spiritual laws are not at war with those of nature, but are 'in perfect harmony with every fresh physical law' that men of daring and courage may discover. 'There is a mighty spirit working among us', he declared.

Yet, in *Yeast* Kingsley introduced Barnakill as a 'Catholic of the Catholics' who wishes, not to smother the 'mighty spirit' of brotherly love, but to exalt it. This spirit, with the universality of the Sermon on the Mount is their catholicism, and it includes all 'isms' whether Protestant or Catholic, High Church or Low. It alone points the way to humanity and thus fulfills the meaning of history.

Often, however, the most God-fearing, the most devout, and the most zealous in good works fall short of self-sacrifice in action. Men are often blinded by an obtruding self. Newman, consciously or otherwise, showed Charles Reding's conversion as stemming from self, rather than divine prompting. Asceticism can be selfish. At the end of the tale, Newman left his convert in a 'temporary cell, so happy in the Present, that he had no thoughts either for the Past or the Future'.

Charles Reding's conversion is personal as a conversion must be. But it results in no sense of social mission. Unlike Paul Tregarva's and Lancelot Smith's conversions in *Yeast*, it offers no vision of a humanity which he may help to save. In contrast with Lancelot Smith, Charles Reding hears no voice impelling him forward to the people. Yet, on Newman's behalf, it may be pointed out that asceticism has always been one of the ways to God, and Newman's portrayal rebukes the indulgence, luxury, and vanity of the English clergy of his day.

Luke's conversion in *Yeast* is not unlike that of Charles Reding in *Loss and Gain*. A minor character introduced as a foil for Paul Tregarva, Luke is made to meet Paul momentarily as each is about to begin his mission. Kingsley cannot reconcile them, however, and as Lancelot turns from one to the other, the opposing converts, though so near, are as far, each from the other, as is the original from its own counterfeit. Lancelot and Paul, who see that their love for each other resembles that between David and Jonathan, know the source of their brotherhood, and happily agree to mutual co-operation; whereas Luke, with his eye on the confessional and his heart already lost to a system of personal salvation, loves neither his friends nor his ruined father.

Kingsley sharply contrasted their respective callings. Sure of his mission, Paul Tregarva sets off to do 'the Lord's work' at the City Mission in Manchester and thus, to oppose the Manchester School whose inhumanity is vividly described by Dickens in *Hard Times*; whereas Luke, already 'converted', turns toward Rome in the full knowledge that his world is crying out for his help. 'It is most fearful', he admits, that a man should be exposed to cholera, typhus, and a host of attendant diseases, simply because he is born into the world an artisan (Ch. XVI, 260). But he can do nothing about it. Just as his unfortunate father 'has sold himself to a system which is its own punishment', so at the close of *Yeast* Kingsley suggests that Luke has committed a 'moral suicide' because he, too, has sold himself to a system.

Systems affect nations as well as individuals and, conversely, a system devised by an individual may affect an entire polity. Maurice and Newman were both imbued with a spirit of reform. Both were disciples of Coleridge and each was the leader of a regenerative movement. Their influences, however, operated in opposite directions. Newman[6] was the 'father of them that look back' while Maurice, looking much further back, was enabled to look both forward and outward in the spirit of the new age. Newman turned to Rome and the system of an infallible Church. Maurice, on the other hand, eschewed all systems and proclaimed the kingdom already established, as having come and still in the process of coming, unfolding gradually, growing organically, as mankind rose upward into humanity. He sought to interpret the kingdom in terms of a total impression on the face of Scripture and history, and as we have seen, he was determined to keep the political life of the English people in union with God and identified with Christ's teaching and, as an interpretation of Maurice, *Yeast* conveys these attitudes.

This is the more important when it is remembered that, as Kingsley was preparing instalments of his novel for *Fraser's*, the Communist Manifesto was being announced to a revolutionary world. It may also be remembered that Ludlow had persuaded Maurice to accept the spiritual leadership of their movement in the belief that the 'socialism' espoused by that manifesto had to be Christianized if it were not to shake Christianity to its foundation, and it cannot be emphasized too often that the socialism put forward by Maurice and Kingsley, with initial clumsiness on Kingsley's part, was Christianity – 'a Gospel from Heaven concerning the relation in which God stands to His creatures, concerning the true law under which He has constituted them'.[7] And this is the essential drift of *Yeast*.

Yeast, then, purports to deal with questions 'fermenting in the minds of the young', and concentrates on the agrarian evils with which Kingsley was familiar. It condemns the Poor Law, the game laws, and the acquisitiveness of the squirearchy. Kingsley contrasted the general well-being of 'the merry brown hares' leaping over 'the crest of the hill' with labourers 'in Christian England,

> Where they cant of a Saviour's name,
> And yet waste men's lives like the vermin's
> For a few more brace of game' (Ch. xi, 173).

Critical of the religious scene, he also inveighed against the laziness of the clergy and deplored the growth of nonconformity. He condemned Calvinism for its materialism in this world and decried Romanism for its emphasis on the next, while both of these and the Church of England were all taken to task for their views on the subject of eternal punishment.[8]

The novel was meant to be frankly instructive, and few writers of the time appreciated the rural climate more accurately than

Kingsley. Surveying the southern counties from his study in Eversley, he drew a vivid and realistic picture of agrarian labourers and painted the darker side of rural life in order to expose the evils breeding Chartism. Unfortunately, his criticism of the establishment often antagonized, and therefore sometimes diminished, the force of his criticism.

The genesis of the novel accounts for most of its major faults. Though a fiction, it shares the tract and the sermon and thus mingles aspects of both. It has been called a long short-story, but it is equally a short novel, so that as a *genre* it leaves something to be desired. Because of the haste with which it was written it lacks finish and is flawed by carelessness in mechanical details. The style occasionally falls into tractarian declamation and is sometimes journalistic and demogogical. Moreover, though the serial in *Fraser's* was curtailed because of its radical bent and its ranting criticism of the clergy and the squirearchy, and though Kingsley had intended to expand it before publishing it as a book, he modified his plans because of complications with *Alton Locke*, and was as relieved as Parker's, his publishers, when they suggested cutting it short. But it meant that *Yeast* was inevitably tentative and inadequate.

Again, 'The Nun's Pool', originally written for, but not published in *Politics for the People*, eventually appeared in the second volume of the *Christian Socialist* after portions of it, as already detailed, had been incorporated in *Yeast*, and this created structural problems. When, under Maurice's supervision, Kingsley actually began to revise the story, he added the theme of Lancelot's tractarian cousin as an essential exposure of system-building, and this complicated the plot. Despite the order imposed on the work by the 'spiritual sequences', the manipulation of three of them caused some confusion in the arrangement of the parts but, above all, much of *Yeast* is autobiographical, dictated by Kingsley's personal experience, which he naturally wished to disguise.

When the novel was published in May, 1851, the *Guardian* immediately identified the writer as the author of *Alton Locke*, which had appeared the previous autumn and, as we already know, the reviewer lost no time in attacking both novels. He condemned *Yeast* out of hand, contending that Kingsley was endeavouring to 'unsettle all practical religious convictions'. Actually, he was 'unsettling' the twisted religious attitudes adopted by many of the country dissenters, who felt that they had no place in the establishment and were troubled by fears of eternal punishment. Unwilling to recognize his aim as directing country folk to practise the simple principles of love and co-operation, the reviewer made his accusations in a manner suggesting that the author was subversive, and although Kingsley hastened to declare that his argument was 'the exact and formal opposite' of this, the criticism nevertheless marked the beginning of a series of bitter attacks, not only on Kingsley himself but, as we have seen, on the movement generally. Unpleasant and slanderous as many of these attacks were, however, they did much to stimulate an interest in Christian Social literature and, ultimately to popularize the name of Charles Kingsley.

Our discussion of *Yeast* may well close with a return to the author whose ideas and literary biography coincide in the novel itself. Maurice had regarded the family as the nucleus of society, which grew into a community that expanded, in turn, into a nation, whose family feeling tempered its relationships with the rest of the world. That Kingsley agreed with his mentor in this as in other matters is amply demonstrated in *Yeast* and, for him whose courtship and marriage were coincident with his conversion, the family was especially significant.

When he and Miss Grenfell met, they immediately fell in love and 'a new life dawned' for both. More than a decade after their meeting Mrs. Kingsley wrote her sister, Mrs. Warre, that Kingsley seemed to grow more devoted to her 'every moment of every day'. 'I never saw such love or imagined it', she said. 'Never, never were we so happy in each other and so utterly knit together'.[9] As for Kingsley himself, he always referred to the day on which they met as their 'real wedding day'.

The important point for *Yeast* is that during this period Kingsley passed through the 'spiritual sequence' to which he had drawn attention in *Fraser's Magazine*. When the pair met on that summer's day in 1839 in Oxfordshire, Kingsley 'was just like his own Lancelot in *Yeast*' and there, for the first time in his life, his 'sad longing expression' met with an 'answering sympathy'.[10]

Kingsley put the parallels in his novel with his usual clear-cut brevity: Lancelot's face 'haunted' Argemone. 'She would convert him.' The biographical implications are clear, and we have already indicated Mrs. Kingsley's role in her husband's conversion. She brought him through 'a dark night of the soul' and guided him into the Church whose 'seals of admission to service' he accepted with joy.

Kingsley wrote but two poems at this time and both of them testify to their united aim. *Palinodia* not only reflects Victorian England but it indicates their will to be at one within it in fulfilling the 'charge' that the Father had laid upon them:

> Through sunless cities, and the weary haunts
> Of smoke-grimed labour, and foul revelry
> My flagging wing has swept. A mateless bird's
> My pilgrimage has been; through sin, and doubt,
> And darkness, seeking love. Oh hear me, Nature!
> Receive me once again: but not alone;
> No more alone, Great Mother! I have brought
> One who has wandered, yet not sinned, like me.
> Upon thy lap, twin children, let us lie;
> And in the lights of thine immortal eyes
> Let our souls mingle, till the Father calls
> To some eternal home the charge He gives.[11]

And if this poem expresses their wish for united endeavour, the little gem below declares the intensity of their dedication:

> Twin stars, aloft in ether clear,
>   Around each other roll away,
> Within one common atmosphere
>   Of their own mutual light and day.
>
> And myriad happy eyes are bent
>   Upon their changeless love alway;
> As, strengthened by their one intent,
>   They pour the flood of life and day.
>
> So we, through this world's waning night,
>   May, hand in hand, pursue our way;
> Shed round us order, love, and light,
>   And shine unto the perfect day.[12]

Yeast, then, is the 'fruit' of their shared mission.

In the novel, Maurice is represented as Barnakill, the prophet. With a humorous twinkle in the use of his fictitious name as a homonym of *barnacle*, a species of wild goose, he read and approved Kingsley's revised chapters before sending them on to John Parker. Maurice suppressed nothing. He told his disciple that, even had he had the power, he should have lacked the courage to express the ideas in it as forthrightly as Kingsley had done.[13] On the other hand, Ludlow, who read the tale as it came out in *Fraser's*, declared that it had the thought, feeling, and interest of any 'first-rate three-volume novel of the day', but he expressed himself as being 'exceedingly frightened' by Kingsley's literary power. As a parson, Kingsley, he said, should write no more novels but, since *Yeast* was already done, he ought to revise it and make it 'ten times pleasanter, thoughtfuller, truer', so as to show the world what 'a great Christian work' a novel could be.[14] As for Kingsley toiling in the night, when he had finished *Yeast*, he had but one comment: 'I think this will explain a good deal of Maurice', he said.[15] So it did, but it explained a good deal more of Charles Kingsley.

Even more, it explained Christian Socialism as well as the novels he was to write. Since each was to be a sermon on moral regeneration, both public and private, *Yeast*, in announcing the themes that permeate the later novels, is seminal for all of them. Built on the phases of religious conversion, this novel provides an underlying framework for them as well; and because the structural sequence derived from Kingsley's personal experience, it also reveals the Victorian integration of life and art and, on the national level, it defines the immediacy of questions vital to all Victorians. In a word, *Yeast* demonstrates the manner in which the novel of purpose brings all aspects of thought into the turbulent stream of life.

CHAPTER 4

Alton Locke

Published in two volumes in August, 1850, *Alton Locke, Tailor and Poet* was sandwiched between 'Yeast' the serial and *Yeast* the book. The most provocative document produced by the Christian socialists, it was written in the midst of controversies, fanned them up the more fiercely when it appeared, and disturbingly gave point to the utterances oral and written that had preceded it, while adding thrust to the *Message of the Church* that was soon to follow. Placards, tracts, Letters to Chartists, and other incunabula including Kingsley's effective and factual *Cheap Clothes and Nasty* had sounded the alarm, but none of these, including the instalments of 'Yeast' in *Fraser's* had caused a comparable storm. Though also propaganda, *Alton Locke* went beyond both pamphleteering and sermonizing to become a full-scale novel of purpose but, partaking of both, it became at once a vital book for the times, and it remains an important work for students of Christian socialism and the period in which it arose.

As literary biography it throws further light on Kingsley, a characteristic man of the time and, as art, it denotes an advance from the veiled autobiography of 'Yeast' to the fictional autobiography of Kingsley's artisan hero. It is convincing because Kingsley made use of biographical material relative to the movement, and the difference between Thomas Cooper, the real-life model, and the fictitious Alton Locke is the difference between dull fact and imaginative fiction. The tale is idealized and as fiction it evoked a more compelling response than factual biography could possibly have done; and simply because of its emotional appeal it is the more potent in seeming to subdue the sermon while simultaneously intensifying its impact. It represents the climactic publication of Kingsley's Parson Lot period, and as such he had a price to pay.

He had indiscreetly pronounced himself a Chartist, and the problem was that under demagogues like Feargus O'Connor they saw force as the only remedy for their ills. Their attempt to take the law into their own hands on the Tenth had actually led Maurice, Kingsley, and Ludlow to start their counter movement. Though more than its Charter, Chartism had never been defined, and in the wake of the Continental revolutions of 1848 the threat against London had seemed equally revolutionary, so that any new movement expressing sympathy with them, however noble the motive, was also regarded with suspicion. Convinced that ends must justify means, the Christian socialists had accepted the challenge, not only to meet Chartists but, by persuasion, to lead them to better feelings. Neither they nor the nation at large understood their aim, and this was the nub of Kingsley's problem as he turned to *Alton Locke*.

The Christian socialists were in a tenuous position. Any kind of association was branded as 'revolutionary Communism'. Moreover, Chartists thirsting for action came to their meetings and it was no easy task to hold the line between moral and physical force. Also, though the workmen were outwardly friendly, the great majority of them continued to mistrust clergymen and lawyers who purported to help them and, in spite of sincere attempts on either side to foil extreme Chartists on the one hand and *Quarterly* reviewers on the other, an indefinable uneasiness dogged their relationships.

Kingsley pressed on, however, and with Chartists reporting their personal problems on every hand, autobiographies were common. One of them, apparently that of John James Bezer, their one-eyed publisher, was printed in the second volume of *The Christian Socialist* as 'The Autobiography of One of the Chartist Rebels of 1848'. Kingsley was thus led to draw his hero from life. He, too, though in fact not a Chartist, would write a Chartist's story as if he were one. This required courage but, bold and undaunted, he proceeded apace.

Alton Locke is a composite of several of the Chartists whom Kingsley had met. Gerald Massey was a working-class poet, but a more likely model was the highly intelligent Robert Lowery, a tailor, who was also a convincing speaker, whose deformed figure seemed to plead for the victims of the slop-shop and the sweater's den.[1] Walter Cooper, a small tailor of 'really considerable attainments',[2] was discovered by Ludlow, taken to hear Maurice preach at Lincoln's Inn, and became the liaison between the Christian socialists and the working-men. He was chosen by the Council of Promoters to organize the first association, that of tailors, and he definitely contributed to the portrait of Alton. Thomas Cooper, the Chartist (1805–92), was the greatest influence in Kingsley's story, however.

Cooper was an ambitious, self-educated man, who had risen from the cobbler's bench to achieve national fame as a Chartist poet and lecturer of no mean powers. Active in the dissemination of their literature, including the *Northern Star* as their official organ, which was edited by William Hill for Feargus O'Connor, he came under the influence of that fiery demagogue himself and, involved in a riot at Hanley for which he was partially responsible, he was arrested and imprisoned on a charge of sedition. While serving his sentence in Stafford gaol, he wrote *The Purgatory of Suicides* (1845), an epic poem that attracted the attention of Kingsley, who eventually reviewed it.[3]

By the time the first instalment of 'Yeast' was ready for Parker's, Kingsley needed a 'friend' to help him realize his 'brotherhood' with working-men:

I want someone like yourself, intimately acquainted with the mind of the working classes [he wrote Cooper], to give me such insight into their life and thoughts, as may enable me to consecrate my powers effectually to their service.[4]

Cooper's reply has been lost, unfortunately, but eighteen months later Kingsley wrote to thank him for his 'history of Chartism', which he hoped to 'reclaim' when next in London.

Alton Locke's story touches Cooper's at many points. Alton, like Cooper, is blest with a superabundance of imagination. Alton, like Cooper, is an author whose collection of poems, *Songs of the Highways*, makes him a poet of the people. Like Cooper, too, Alton is reared by a dissenting, widowed mother, is bound over to an apprenticeship (though in the tailoring, rather than the cobbling, trade), is largely self-educated, grows atheistical, writes for radical papers, and attempts to 'rise in life'. As Thomas Cooper was encouraged by a second-hand book-seller in Chancery Lane, so Alton finds guidance and encouragement in Saunders Mackaye, whose book-shop is the focal-point in Kingsley's novel; and as Alton addresses a Chartist meeting, is involved in a riot, brought to trial and imprisoned, so Cooper, too, had experienced all of these ordeals. The parallels are obvious, but as Kingsley was writing fiction, there are naturally variations and adaptations in his text, and Alton's story may be compared with *The Life of Thomas Cooper*, written by himself and published in 1872, twenty years after Kingsley's novel.

As *Alton Locke* was growing out of the Christian Socialist Movement so, too, by a happy coincidence, the *Morning Chronicle* was publishing authentic background information for it. On 24 September, 1849,[5] there appeared the first of a series of leaders describing the pockets of pestilence in the London slums and these, together with two articles by Henry Mayhew describing conditions among working tailors and printed in the same paper on 14 and 18 December respectively,[6] provided Kingsley with too much information to leave him altogether master of himself. Walter Cooper, who knew the conditions among the tailors, attested to its reliability, and urged Kingsley to visit the area for himself.

Within the month Kingsley and two of his friends, George Walsh, a medical man who was studying cholera, and Charles Mansfield, who was interested in chemistry, visited Jacob's Island, Bermondsey. They were appalled. An open sewer ran between the backs of the shambling houses. Crossing one of the 'crazy and rotting bridges over the reeking ditch', they saw 'heavy bubbles' rising from the scum-covered water, and the 'swollen carcasses of dead animals, almost bursting with putrefaction'. Built on piles, many of the houses stood directly over the sewer and here, 'with the heavy stench of death' rising through the floor-boards, human beings, as the *Chronicle* explained, slept night after night 'until the last sleep of all'.[7] While they lived, however, the sewer was their only source of drinking water.

If Kingsley had been excited by the *Chronicle* descriptions, the slum itself drove him to frenzy. It was like living through the

Bristol riots again. Back in Chelsea, he wrote a number of letters to rouse Christian socialists and others who could help and, these despatched, he turned impetuously to his tract. *Cheap Clothes and Nasty* exposed the injustice, privation, and distress among tailors, thus causing a storm of mingled anger and protest.

In it, Kingsley distinguished between the honourable and the dishonourable trades. In the first, the work was done 'on the premises and at good wages', under the supervision of a master-tailor. In the second, piece-work was taken home to be done speedily 'at the very lowest possible prices'. This meant re-letting parts of the work for a profit, to contractors or middle-men called 'sweaters' who, in turn, handed it on for their profit to a 'sweater's sweater', and so on; in the end, the poor tailor who did the bulk of the work received almost nothing.[8] Viciously competitive, the system operated to reduce wages, extend working hours, and drive the workers to prey upon one another. *Alton Locke* presupposes a knowledge of this inhuman practice, the driest factual details of which Kingsley did not transpose into his novel; and though his book roused concern and stimulated improvement, the condition among east-end tailors was still a 'burning controversy' in 1889.[9]

As the novel begins, Alton Locke is sitting in a ship's cabin writing the story of his own unhappy life. He, the hero, has become a tailor, a working-class poet, and a Chartist who turns to physical force but who, in the course of time, has a change of heart and repents. As the ship rolls on toward America, 'the wild waters slipping past the cabin window', his past flows from his pen onto the paper before him as he records all 'for the sake of the rich who read, and the poor who suffer'. Though pioneering the way for other emigrants, Alton like Moses of old is destined never to enter the promised land. When the ship is berthed in Galveston, John Crossthwaite, who was transported in the same ship, finds Alton dead at his desk, the ink 'not yet dry' on the last sheet of the heart-rending tale he has written. That tale is Kingsley's *Alton Locke*.

Knowing that his book would be thought radical, Kingsley was not surprised when Parker's refused it. They had sustained losses in business and reputation by issuing *Politics for the People* and serializing 'Yeast', and they dared not risk further recriminations just then. Under the sponsorship of Carlyle, Kingsley therefore turned to Chapman and Hall, who were themselves cautious and questioned him about his manuscript. He wrote to explain: 'My book does not, as you seem to think, deal principally with the slop and sweating question', he told them. He had introduced the tailors and their problems only 'incidentally'. The principal part of *Alton Locke*, on the contrary, was none other than 'the struggles of a poor genius', his 'temptations to political discontent', and his ultimate acceptance of 'real Christianity' as the 'permanent remedy' for them.[10]

Kingsley meant that the 'spiritual sequence' he had asked his readers to find in *Yeast* was also present in *Alton Locke*. As St. Paul's prevision had been followed by a period of darkness, so Alton suffers a protracted 'dark night of the soul' within the conversion sequence, and this adumbrates Kingsley's structural design, except that there is little evidence of any intuitive prevision preceding Alton's darkness. Kingsley also uses the concept in terms of the Biblical narrative, which reveals history as a con- tinuous process of alternating obedience and disobedience in turning to, then from, God; and he makes his hero's story a parallel to that of national history. Though dwelling at length on Alton's perversion, Kingsley constrained his back-sliding hero to return to God, and whether regarded as a dark night within the conversion sequence, or as a perversion working itself out before turning again to right thinking and right action, *Alton Locke* is the history of a stiff-necked hero.

Of the forty-one chapters in *Alton Locke* the second volume of the first edition began with the chapter entitled 'An Emersonian Sermon'. The division is a structural sign-post, but the thematic divisions suggested by Kingsley himself are more instructive. The slop-and-sweating theme is ancillary, as Kingsley explained, but it is essential to the principal theme as well. The account of Alton's struggles and temptations – his perversion – runs from the beginning of the novel to the end of the thirty-fifth chapter, when the story of his conversion to 'real Christianity' begins. The first five chapters, though narrating Alton's early life, introduce a counterfeit conversion, and thus form a contrasting parallel with the last five, which are introduced by the curious and transitional chapter, 'Dreamland', a mythic, historico-evolutionary treatment of developing life on this planet.

The tailor theme has important ramifications. Kingsley uses it, first, as a vehicle for the expression of Alton's discontent which expresses itself in Chartism and, secondly, as a means of bringing his hero face to face with the two opposing but related aspects of it – moral, as opposed to physical force. To his apprenticeship in the tailoring trade Alton owes his acquaintance with Mackaye, the advocate of moral force and, even more directly, with Crossthwaite, the proponent of physical force.

Meditating on the shape of his novel, Kingsley, like Coleridge, saw 'pairs of poles' as correlative rather than contradictory, each giving the other 'a real standing ground' in a reconciling equilibrium. When Alton first meets the two men, they appear to be friendly and are secretly working together for the Cause. They are thus in balance and Alton cannot possibly know that a serious difference of approach is finally to divide them.

Neither can the reader; and the major fault in the novel is that this growing difference is scarcely in evidence until, suddenly, Mackaye refuses to sign Crossthwaite's petition. It is largely inherent in the portrayal of Mackaye, and will be dealt with below. But the failure to distinguish between these two aspects of Chartism was a serious problem of the age and, by a curious coincidence, Kingsley's novel retains something of the confusion of his contemporaries.

As the representative of moral force Sandy Mackaye is the most fully developed character in the book, and, thus the most human. In Mackaye, who speaks in a Scottish dialect, Kingsley gives us a portrait of Carlyle whose writings constitute the old man's favourite reading, give him an unfailing fund of pithy prophecies, and provide his inscrutable philosophy. Contradictory though his characterization is, Kingsley's portrayal suggests an unyielding rectitude born of combined Old Testament authoritarianism and retributive warnings.

The centre of moral-force Chartism, Mackaye's book-shop is the focal point of the novel. 'Piled and fringed outside and in' with all kinds of books, drawings, and bric-à-brac, the shop bespeaks Mackaye's personality, while the rows of pamphlets and political caricatures suspended from the low ceiling 'like clothes hung out to dry' emphatically proclaim his prejudices. Bentham and Malthus, the High-Church party and the Manchester school are all anathema, but the working-men enjoy his unqualified approval, and Alton soon learns that their Cause alone keeps him alive. That Alton is allowed to share the old man's lodgings indicates that, in the beginning, he is firmly anchored with the forces representing insistent but peaceful reform. To this shop with its refuge near the fireplace 'just big enough to hold his arm-chair and a table, book-strewn . . . and garnished with odds and ends' – to this 'book alluvium' come the major characters in the novel: Crosssthwaite, the physical-force Chartist; Mr. Wigginton, the dissenting chaplain, who advises Alton's mother and eventually marries his sister, Susan; the aristocratic but social-working Eleanor, Lady Ellerton; the conspiratorial spy, 'Bower or Power'; and, of course, Alton.

From Mackaye comes the finest speech in the novel. On the eve of the Tenth, when the conflict between Crossthwaite and Mackaye, between physical and moral force, comes into the open, Mackaye refuses to sign the insurrectionary petition and Crossthwaite, threatening to report him to the Convention, is shown as the twisted bully that he is. Before suffering a stroke and disappearing from the novel, Mackaye lashes out with a retort suggesting both the folly of the insurgents and the highly respectable history of the moral-force movement.

In this speech, Kingsley makes the purpose of his novel abundantly clear: he, too, is preaching traditional moral reform and, he, too, is casting defiance in the teeth of the insurgents:

'Do, laddie! do, then! [is Sandy's retort to Crossthwaite's threat] An' tell 'em this, too – . . . – them that stone the prophets, an' quench the Spirit o' God, and love a lie, an' them that mak the same – them that think to bring about the reign o' love an' britherhood wi' pikes an' vitriol bottles, murther an' blasphemy – tell 'em that ane o' fourscore years and mair – ane that has grawn grey in the people's cause – that sat at the feet o'

Cartwright, an' knelt by the death-bed o' Rabbie Burns – ane that cheerit Burdett as he went to the Touer, an' spent his wee earnings for Hunt an' Cobbett – ane that beheld the birth-shriek o' a new-born world – ane that while he was yet a callant saw Liberty afar off, an' seeing her was glad, as for a bonny bride, an' followed her through the wilderness for three-score weary waeful years – sends them the last message that e'er he'll send on airth: tell 'em that they're the slaves o' warse than priests and kings – the slaves o' their ain lusts an' passions – (Ch. XXXIII, 350).

The story of Alton as a rising poet is part of Kingsley's main theme – the struggles of a poor genius – but two aspects of it may be mentioned here. It carries the moral of the book and gives Kingsley an opportunity to introduce a touching poem. Possessed of a powerful imagination, keenly sensitive to beauty, and deeply appreciative of all that culture and refinement mean, the poor Alton may well write a poem for the wealthy Lillian Winnstay. But readers are not surprised at the pathos that haunts the minor music of *The Sands of Dee*, and its setting in the novel gives it added poignancy. By his juxtaposition of wealth with poverty Kingsley cuts to the quick of human feeling, for Alton's poem is itself a gulf between antipodal polarities, between Lillian's shallow mind and Alton's poetic genius.

Kingsley indicates much untapped but redeemable talent among the lower classes, but he ignores the mediatorial role of education in bridging the gulf between them and he assumes that labourers, when made sensible of 'the dignity of work', will remain contented labourers, and that anyone attempting to rise above his class knowingly 'leaves God's path for his own'.[11] This is precisely Alton's feeling when he defers to Dean Winnstay and agrees to delete 'certain passages of a strong political tendency' from his manuscript. Though these constitute 'the very pith and marrow' of his poems, he weakly abandons his convictions for a fleeting moment of triumph before being goaded, first, by Lillian's cousin Eleanor, then, by his own class and the popular press, and, above all, by his own conscience. He is 'a flunky and a dastard'. It *is* a matter of conscience, and for his cowardice he deserves to be cast down. Had he stood up to his convictions he would have risen in his own self-esteem and gained the approval of all, regardless of his class.

But *The Sands of Dee* speaks for itself:

> 'O Mary, go and call the cattle home,
>   And call the cattle home,
>   And call the cattle home,
>   Across the sands o' Dee;'
> The western wind was wild and dank wi' foam,
>   And all alone went she.
>
> The creeping tide came up along the sand,
>   And o'er and o'er the sand,
>   And round and round the sand,
>   As far as eye could see;
> The blinding mist came down and hid the land:
>   And never home came she.
>
>   . . .
>
> They rowed her in across the rolling foam,
>   The cruel crawling foam,
>   The cruel hungry foam,
>   To her grave beside the sea:
> But still the boatmen hear her call the cattle home,
>   Across the sands o' Dee (Ch. XXVI, 267).

Bespeaking the transience of life and echoing the vanity of worldly success, the poem fails to reach Lillian. In the social context of the novel, Kingsley is suggesting an analogy between the cruelty of nature and the social system imposed upon the poor. Unless the rule of the carefree rich is tempered by the milk of human kindness, the working people – the humble Marys of this world – may be swept away altogether, and with them, the whole fabric of society. Time, like tide, waits for no man and reform is imperative for the 'day of the Lord' is at hand.

Since Kingsley aimed to put the case for personal reform in the strongest possible terms, he illustrated conversion by exposing its opposite. As *Yeast* included a false conversion in Luke's story, so *Alton Locke* boasts two of them. The first, a commonplace phenomenon in the nineteenth-century, is that of cousin George. The second concentrates on the religious system in which Alton and his sister, Susan, were brought up, and to which she is 'converted'. George's conversion is closely related to other themes in the novel, particularly the principal one, and the result of Susan's kind of experience is exemplified in their mother, whose conversion is portrayed in the first five chapters, where it contrasts with Alton's, in the concluding five.

George's 'conversion' is a matter of expediency. He has long since abandoned the strict and unappealing code of the dissenters. A child of this world, he turns enthusiastically to the comfort of the Establishment and, having resolved to take holy orders, airily informs Alton that

> it is the only method yet discovered for turning a snob . . . into a gentleman. . . . If you are once a parson, all is safe. Be you who you may before, from that moment you are a gentleman. No one will offer an insult. You are good enough for any man's society (Ch. XII, 147).

Lacking all sense of vocation, he unhesitatingly signs the Thirty-nine Articles and, counting on a grace supposedly given at ordination he plans to carry out the 'Church system' as the only way of rising in the world:

> You can be a friend, . . . if you like, to the highest women in the land; and if you have person, manners, and common sense, marry one of them into the bargain, Alton my boy (Ch. XIII, 147),

he concludes smugly. Alton's evil genius, the personable George does just that, unscrupulously outwitting Alton for the hand of Lillian Winnstay. His 'coarse and selfish ambition' declares itself more and more flagrantly as the novel proceeds.

Kingsley thus rebuked the pharisaical clergy, who were destroying the Church from within. Though Alton does not actually accuse George of hypocrisy, he feels that his cousin has never known what 'believing' means, that like hundreds of his kind he has never felt the 'shining flame of intense conviction . . . for which he would not fear to die'. In other words, George has no mission, and this is disturbing because he is deliberately and unashamedly self-seeking. The poor have no place in his scheme of things, and this is the more deplorable because the 'established' clergy are in a position to help the poor and teach the rich their duty more effectively than any, had they a genuine mission to do so.

As for Alton's mother, she makes her appearance at the beginning of the novel, 'a sensible sinner' but 'not without assurance of her election', and as one, therefore, already 'converted'. A widow, she has abandoned a group of Independents for the 'higher doctrine' of a Baptist sect, whose antinomian attitudes are based on contemporary interpretations of Calvin. Pious, dutiful, and full of sober good works, she dare not think of Jesus as loving indiscriminately, for all, including her own progeny, are 'children of the devil' until they are 'converted'. Those especially chosen by God, His elect, will be saved, she believes, but all others are reprobate and doomed to eternal punishment.

The well-meaning woman moves 'by rule and method' and keeps 'the strictest watch' over the morality of her children, whose gods are 'hell, the rod, the ten commandments, and public opinion'. In her sixteenth year Susan goes through 'the process of conversion' and is 'looked upon at the chapel as an especially gracious professor' of 'vital Christianity'. When Alton meets her several years later, she is about to marry 'that dear man of God', Mr. Wigginton, who is being 'removed to the work of the Lord in Manchester'. Soured, and inhibited, she has become a fit helpmate for one devoted to that school which successfully swept away 'all traces of any restriction or guidance in the employment of money'.[12] Her mission, like her husband's, is the gospel of getting on.

Alton on the other hand, when once exposed to the Babylonian world, loses what little faith he has, and when he is taken to task by Mr. Wigginton for reading Milton and other 'heathen authors', he rebels. 'If I am elect, I shall be saved whatever I do', he declares vehemently, 'and if I am not, I shall be damned whatever I do'. When his mother warns him about election and his need for 'conversion', he falls into 'a fit of rage' and bursts out:

Religion? Nobody believes in it. The rich don't; or they wouldn't fill their churches up with pews, and shut the poor out, all the time they are calling them brothers. ... No more do the tradespeople believe in it ... and grind the last farthing out of the poor creatures who rent their wretched and stinking houses. And as for the workmen – they laugh at it all, ... (Ch. v, 58).

For this volley of unregenerate scepticism, his mother, her piety outraged, dutifully orders him to leave her house, and Alton is thus thrown upon the world.

Kingsley's delineation of dissenters in *Alton Locke* is particularly unflattering, and although he added a conciliating footnote for sensitive readers (Ch. III, 40 n.), it is not unreasonable to suppose that he was writing from experience and that his sketches of Alton's mother and her narrow chaplain are not greatly over-drawn. He had found a great prevalence of the Baptist form of dissent in his parish and, founded as it was on 'supra-lapsarian Calvinistic dogmas' which the sect regarded as Scriptural, he had sought Maurice's advice on ways of retrieving them.[13] Under their system, as Alton not unreasonably told Mr. Wigginton, a man starving in this world and expecting eternal punishment in the next felt little compulsion either to conduct himself morally or to improve himself socially. Kingsley argued that the individualism of Calvinism, like that of Popery, failed to square with 'the facts of Christianity'. Their systems, in failing to recognize a fraternal life and a corporate history as represented by Adam and Jacob could not Christianize working-men.[14]

Maurice and Kingsley both felt that the clergy of every school had to face the dangers inherent in over-emphasizing eternal punishment. In attempting to speak for all, Maurice was to incur the ire of the Establishment and to write himself out of his divinity professorship at King's College, London, with his *Theological Essays*, in the last of which he was to declare that Christ's earthly life had assured the ultimate redemption of all mankind. He therefor dismissed at one blow a doctrine which many believed to encourage atheism and philosophical determinism. It was time to correct the 'darkling error' into which Alton and his class had wandered; and equally time that a doctrine which sanctioned the astute profiteering of the Manchester school at the expense of the 'reprobate' should be exposed as the self-seeking materialism that it was.

What, then, of the 'darkling error' into which Alton wanders when thrown upon the world? Since the struggles of the poor genius have already emerged in connexion with the ancillary themes, it only remains to follow 'his temptations to political discontent' in terms of the sequence on which Kingsley built his novel, that is, in terms of a protracted perversion.

Alton is obviously in a consciously wrong and unhappy state,[15] and his journey from his mother's door begins on the road to despair as Kingsley clearly indicates his hero's growing defection. Alton begins by becoming a Chartist and is soon tainted with radicalism and subversion. Gradually he abandons Mackaye's moral-force teaching for that of the radical Crossthwaite, and this is followed by a riot in which he is involved and for which he is brought to trial and imprisonment. Far from inducing him to take another road, prison darkens his mind and, emerging with a thirst for revenge, he assists French and Irish conspirators with plans for the rising on the Tenth. Its collapse brings him to despair.

Kingsley uses imagery of darkness to establish his perversion pattern. In exchanging his home for a tailor's workroom Alton leaves a 'narrow' for a 'darker' cage. Crossthwaite's 'fierce earnestness' cloaks much, and he loses no time in sowing seeds of darkness in his protégé, ultimately urging him and his friends to strike work. Mackaye, too, is shrouded in mystery, his shop being 'so dark' that only he can see to read without a light. Even the window is 'blocked up' with bundles and books, which are in 'the wildest confusion'. Kingsley consistently pursues imagery of this kind throughout this sequence, concluding with the 'black wherry' that glides coffin-like from beneath the arch of Waterloo bridge on which Alton stands on the brink of a suicidal jump into the dark waters below.

A history of Alton's life, the novel also records a second aspect of his perversion, a mistake made in the Dulwich Gallery, which also marks a 'turning-point' in his career. The aristocratic Dean Winnstay with Lillian, and her cousin, Eleanor Staunton are also in the gallery and, as Alton gazes at Guido's St. Sebastian, Eleanor, observing his deep feeling, speaks to him about it. As he turns to reply, his poet's soul full of the painting, his eye is caught before he can answer, by an 'apparition', the lovely Lillian, with whom he immediately falls in love. Eleanor is ignored.

The mistake is vital. Establishing the plot, it hastens Alton down his darkening road. Busy with good works among the poor, Eleanor marries Lynedale, Lord Ellerton, whose model estates engross her attention. They resemble those planned by Dorothea Brooke in *Middlemarch*, except that hers remain a dream. Eleanor is a woman of action, who quietly works through Mackaye to help Alton, whereas Lillian is shallow and cold, engrossed in the narrow pursuits of her own world and, lacking sincerity, fails Alton at his trial by deferring to his cousin. Pursuing the very people he decries, Alton has mistaken the dream for the reality and has fallen in love with an 'apparition', a phantom which he pursues in self-imposed blindness.

Thus Kingsley plots tensions between opposing societies. Just as Alton chooses Crossthwaite and physical force instead of Mackaye and moral force, so now he chooses the socialite rather than the protagonist of Christian brotherhood. A further conflict between the supposedly idle rich and the dehumanized poor, and an additional tension between the working-class Alton and his 'rising' cousin completes the structural framework.

When the plans for the Tenth have fizzled out Alton comes into the dark night of his discontent. Forsaken by family and friends, deserted by Lillian and feeling that he has lost his honour and self-respect, he deserts even himself. On Waterloo bridge he looks over the rail into 'the desolate night' and, poised on the brink of suicide, his attention is distracted and he involuntarily asserts his better self to save another, who is also in despair. The darkness that follows is not that of death, but a mental collapse into the delirium of brain-fever. So ends Alton's perversion sequence.

Alton's acceptance of 'real Christianity' need not detain us. When he emerges from the night of perversion and delirium, he discovers that he has passed 'through the painful gate of birth into another life', and his new phase begins with 'infinite submission and humility'. He is now ripe for conversion, or more properly, for the systolic aspect of it, which now replaces the diastolic regression.

To Lady Ellerton, the prophetess of Maurice's idealism, goes the credit for Alton's change, for the 'real Christianity' that Kingsley declares to be the only remedy for temptations to political discontent is now introduced by her. Readings from Tennyson, Thomas à Kempis, and the Psalms induce a desire for atonement and with that, the determination to emulate Christ, the great Hero and Reformer, whose mission on earth now becomes Alton's. God has called him to do a great work, for he is to love his brothers with all his faculties. He must 'live and die struggling for their rights, endeavouring to make them . . . fit to be electors, senators, kings, and priests to God and to His Christ' (Ch. XL, 429). This is 'the Chartism of the future', which Kingsley defines as the mission of every Christian man and, in so doing, he explains what he had meant by declaring himself a Church of England parson, and a Chartist. He was not a Chartist, however, but a Christian socialist preaching Christianity.

Lady Ellerton's message ought to have come from the clergy and in assigning it to her Kingsley extends a rebuke to them and a compliment to woman as a civilizing influence in society. That she is also aristocratic is deliberate on his part, for it was the age of Elizabeth Fry (1780–1845) and Florence Nightingale (1820–1910); and of Octavia Hill (1838–1912), who helped the Christian socialists among the London poor. These women did more for the workers than they could do for themselves.

Structurally, Kingsley badly mishandled this episode. Since Eleanor plays a minor role in the novel and is unsympathetically portrayed, it comes as grotesquely contrived that she should have saved the recalcitrants. Their reclamation comes upon the reader, not as an integral part of the story, but as something outside it. The changes in Alton and, more particularly, in Crossthwaite are too sudden to be convincing. To have been effective, her theology ought to have been integrated into the narrative so that her teaching, like that of Mackaye, could have operated in its own right.[16]

The present arrangement of the novel gives undue prominence to the diastolic at the expense of the systolic movement, although Kingsley undoubtedly intended to make Alton's return to godliness the redeeming and exultant climax of his tale. In *Alton Locke* Kingsley is really saying what Wordsworth told Thomas Cooper some years after his release from prison. 'You were quite right,' he said, adding that there was 'nothing unreasonable' in the Charter, but that it was 'the foolish attempt at physical force' that had caused Cooper's downfall.[17] Kingsley had read *The Excursion* and had assured his wife that the poet was also 'a preacher and prophet of God's new and divine philosophy'.[18] As feeling, love attracts while selfishness repels; and social stability depends ultimately on a just reconciliation of opposing elements.[19]

Everyone agrees that *Alton Locke* 'meddles with too many questions', is 'too political' in some places, and 'too theological' in others.[20] Though Kingsley had taken 'a year to write it and ten to think it', he might well have added another for rigid excision. Quite unwell during much of the writing, he reveals signs of serious confusion, and it may be questioned whether, without the aid of his wife who acted as his amanuensis, the book would ever have seen the light of day. The canvas is too crowded, and Carlyle described it as 'a fervid creation still left half chaotic'.

In short, no sooner had the movement got under way than Kingsley suffered a nervous breakdown. His collapse had been imminent when he had returned to Eversley after the exciting activities immediately following the Tenth. In addition to his usual parish work he had taken on the onerous task of preparing monthly instalments of 'Yeast'. He had been doing too much, but as he rested in Devon he had continued to dream about the autobiography of a Cockney Poet that was to become *Alton Locke*.

His plan to promote reform by exposing the penurious and circumscribed life of a Cockney tailor was excellent for purposes of propaganda, but it was unfortunately attended with difficulties. A liberal clergyman, he had embraced Christian socialism and was preaching brotherhood. Yet he had found himself planning a Chartist novel, as we have seen, and he had struck up an acquaintance with Cooper, who was known to be a radical with a prison record. Keenly aware of his embarrassing position, he had nevertheless clung stubbornly to his plan, but not without undue nervous fatigue.

Even the practical side of the venture had been disturbing. The descent into a Chartist world of filth and poverty had caused the sensitive Kingsley deep suffering and, social distinctions being what they were, had also made him the butt of criticism among his own class and in his profession.[21] His camaraderie with Cooper, though possibly excusable on literary grounds, was not on any other, his friends had felt. A writer might look into working-class conditions, including those of Chartists. But Cooper, an atheist in 1848, was teaching a deterministic Straussism alien both to Kingsley and the Church, and – after his conversion by Kingsley in 1856, when he abruptly terminated his lectures – to Cooper himself. The connexion had therefore strengthened the charges of radicalism against Kingsley, and his determination to persevere had only prolonged his nervous prostration. But by February, 1849, he had felt much better and had written Ludlow that his Autobiography was being revealed 'rapidly and methodically' 'from above'; that only his 'folly' could spoil it.[22]

Although the revelations were soon less rapid and methodical than they had apparently been at the beginning, Kingsley did not spoil his story, but it is seriously out of focus. A few examples will illustrate the point, and the first has already been set forth with considerable detail. The emphasis in the book falls on perversion when, in fact, Kingsley wished to stress the need for personal reform from within. Again, though *Alton Locke*, as we have attempted to demonstrate, is actually publishing Christian socialism, the greater part of the text puts the case, unfortunately, not only for Chartism, but for bellicosity as essential for the achievement of it.

The change from moral reform to force comes too suddenly and without the needed preparation by the author. Almost without warning, as what was originally the first volume of the novel draws to a close, Alton surprisingly declares that Mackaye has 'nothing positive, after all, to advise or propound'. Alton suddenly sees his wisdom as

apophthegms and maxims, utterly impracticable, too often merely negative, as was his creed, which though he refused to be classed with any sect, was really a somewhat undefined Unitarianism – or rather Islamism. He could say, with the old Moslem, 'God is great – who hath resisted his will?' And he believed what he said, and lived manful and pure, reverent and self-denying, by that belief, . . . But it was not enough. . . . He felt it so himself; for he grew daily more and more cynical, more and more hopeless about the prospects of his class and of all humanity (Ch. xx, 212).

On the eve of the Tenth when Alton has quite abandoned himself to physical force, the old man suffers a stroke and disappears from the novel.

Quite simply, Thomas Cooper's story is allowed to tell too much of Alton Locke's, and though the novel was the most important work issued by the Christian socialists during their active period between 1848–54, and though it did and indeed does assert Christian principles of association, it is none the less generally referred to as Kingsley's Chartist novel. Many of these difficulties could have been avoided by a fresh arrangement of some of the episodes so as to shift the emphasis.

The most serious fault concerns the portrayal of Mackaye, and in order to understand this we must return to Kingsley's biography. The interval spent in London on the way to Eversley from Ilfracombe, when the novel was evidently half done, seems to have given Kingsley a serious jolt from which he fully recovered only when he had finished it. *Alton Locke* was the battlefield of his conflict and the writing of the novel itself the therapy that clarified his own thinking.

Kingsley liked Carlyle's 'tangible original language'. It cut through the conventional pulpit oratory of both Evangelicals and Tractarians and, transcending party interests, roused his readers to the ills of society as that of the clergy, he thought, did not. *The French Revolution* and *Past and Present* argued strongly for God's righteous government of the world and formed an excellent introduction to Maurice's seminal work, *The Kingdom of Christ*; while *Chartism*, vociferous in the name of justice, put the case for reform with irresistible appeal for an excitable and impulsive young man like Kingsley. Bent on practical reform, he had gone on to Christian socialism and, in his enthusiasm, he had taken it for granted that Carlyle and Maurice were men of like mind. He had read both, had associated the teaching of both with his personal vision, and had grown to love and revere the qualities peculiar to each. Both were fighting for the same cause and, on the face of it, both were preaching the same creed.

Though dashing about London had relieved Kingsley's nervous tension, a diversity of interests had conspired to renew and intensify his confusion. He had listened to Feargus O'Connor's impractical scheme for a Chartist–Co-operative Land Company. He had visited Carlyle, whose doctrine was increasingly one of mights as rights. He was torn between Ludlow's practical plans for associations modelled on the *Associations Ouvrières* in Paris and Maurice's Christian but impractical idealism. Now, too, arose the distinction between *socialism* and *democracy* that was to come to a head in *The Duty of the Age*. Above all, Kingsley now saw fundamental differences between Maurice and Carlyle, and all these problems had their effect on the Cockney autobiography, which was still churning in his mind.

Kingsley's Chartist novel is also his Carlylean novel. Carlyle's name is scattered ubiquitously throughout the pages of the book. His pithy and prophetic sayings issue, sometimes from the author himself, sometimes from Alton, generally from Mackaye whose portrait is that of Carlyle and, confusingly, from Crossthwaite. Though depicted as opposing forces in the novel, Mackaye and Crossthwaite are actually two aspects of Carlyle, Mackaye representing the earlier Calvinist, and Crossthwaite, the later but incipient protagonist of force. Crossthwaite has erected his insurrectionary plans on a doctrine of mights as rights, as Alton assures us at the close of Chapter XXXIII, and this doctrine is inherent in Carlyle's *Chartism*,[23] a doctrine which, Kingsley saw, must be utterly rejected.

On the other hand, although Mackaye symbolizes moral force, he unfortunately represents the equally unsatisfactory unsocial doctrines of Judaic-Calvinism. He is at one with Alton's mother (Ch. XXXIV, 357). Like her, he lives by a God who is a fountain of justice rather than just. As Crossthwaite must be set aside, so also must Mackaye. As the representative of both Crossthwaite and Mackaye, Carlyle, though the prophet of the age, must go too. Maurice is Kingsley's man.

Stripped of its fictional disguise, Alton's account of his deterioration (Ch. XX, 212) is much more than the explanation of a perverted hero turning from moral to physical force. It is heavily weighted with authorial overtones. Seeing clearly what *Christian* socialism means, Kingsley, in a speech of considerable bravery tinged with temerity even though screened through his fictional creation, Alton Locke, reveals that his mind has cleared, and that he has taken his stand (Ch. xx, 212). That Carlyle, who apparently never looked in his own glass, should have missed his own castigation is as incredible as his 'wonder' at the way Kingsley had 'contrived to manage' Saunders Mackaye.

Kingsley, however, meant what he said. In a letter to Maurice he was to speak of an evening spent, in company with Froude and Parker, in the presence of Carlyle. 'Never heard I a more foolish outpouring of Devil's Doctrine', he wrote Maurice, 'raving cynicism [and] . . . all the ferocity of the old Pharisee without Isaiah's prophecy of mercy and redemption – the notion of sympathy with sinners denounced. . . .' Thoroughly disillusioned, he is nevertheless quite certain where his allegiance lies. 'Though I never can forget what he has taught me', he concluded, 'where should I have been if you had not brought me *the* step beyond him?'[24] In his preface to the undergraduates of Cambridge in the 1862 edition of *Alton Locke* Kingsley attributed the readily noticeable improvement in English society to the High-Church movement, to Dr. Arnold, and to Maurice. Carlyle is not mentioned.

The battlefield of Kingsley's conflict, his book was also the garden-plot of his transformation. During the writing of *Alton Locke* the impetuous youth had gradually mellowed into the more cautious man. In the beginning he had written with a fiery zeal that knew only certainty and no doubt. The world, he should change in a twinkling. But in the heat of the day he tempered his steel and dampened his fire and, chastened, had continued 'in fear and trembling'. At the book's close, he found himself a conservative clergyman rising against the background of his birth into the idealism of the Establishment.

When *Alton Locke* came out, the *Record* led the attacks against it, but Maurice studiously avoided a public comment of any kind. He felt that anything he might say was bound to be misconstrued, either by the working-men or the Establishment, and the implication is that he had serious reservations.[25] Carlyle, on the other hand, pronounced authoritatively on 'both the black of it and the white' and, on 31 October, 1850, in thanking Kingsley for his copy, 'stipulated' that Kingsley should see him when next in Chelsea.[26]

No doubt Kingsley dutifully did so, but he informed Maurice, 'I have no counsellor save you, and want one, I think, more than ever'.[27] On the 30th, a day before the date of Carlyle's epistle, Kingsley had written, 'My dearest Master, I hear you are come home. If so, for God's sake come down and see me. . . .'[28] Whether Maurice went, we do not know. But we do know that he agreed to supervise the re-writing of *Yeast*, and that, as the flood of bitter criticism broke upon *Alton Locke*, he gently guided his disciple away from contemporary embroilments into the peaceful paths of history. Under Maurice's direction, Kingsley was already reading for *Hypatia*. Whatever we may think of *Alton Locke* as a novel of purpose, however, it floodlights its author as a man of the time, who presented his conflicts with an immediacy that few others had achieved.

CHAPTER 5

Hypatia

In financial difficulties in 1851, Kingsley had to augment the living at Eversley and, although this inevitably prevented him from devoting much time to the non-paying *Christian Socialist*, he assured Maurice that he intended to continue fighting the Philistines. For two years he had wished to tell the story of Hypatia, the Neoplatonic philosopher who had been murdered by the Christians, and in so doing, to show how the old world could instruct the new.

It seemed to him that many of his contemporaries were like the Christians of Hypatia's time while still others, who considered themselves to be Christians, were really Hypatian Neoplatonists in their aversion from anything approaching a gospel for the 'merely human masses'. In his view, both groups had confused the nature of reason. Substituting an intellectual for a moral Christianity,[1] they had reduced the imagination, which Coleridge equated with faith in matters theological, to the level of the understanding. *Hypatia*, then, would depict Christianity as 'the only democratic creed', and would show philosophy – whether in the fifth or the nineteenth century – to be 'exclusively aristocratic':[2] it would show, indeed, that a 'new foe' in Victorian England wore the 'old face' of Hypatian Neoplatonism.

Kingsley had read the account of Hypatia's martyrdom in the *Ecclesiastical History* of Socrates Scholasticus,[3] and the awful scene of her death had risen before him with all the clarity of a dream that nevertheless remained a bright reality in his imagination. He would invest the dry facts of history with the emotions of living men and women, and in the background he would paint the confused and motley life of Alexandria as it ebbed and flowed around them during Hypatia's brief hour upon the stage. Hypatia and her world should live again in all the brightness with which they filled his own mind, and thus would he teach his own generation the meaning of those times for their own.

[84]

Other sources were not wanting. John Toland was the first English writer to revive Hypatia's story in *Tetradymus* (1820), but Gibbon had drawn heavily upon Socrates' *History* for his account, and Kingsley certainly consulted Chapter XLVII of *The Decline and Fall of the Roman Empire*. He also had access to *The Letters of Synesius* as well as those of Isidore;[4] and he was familiar with Augustine's *Confessions* and *The City of God*, both of which illustrated the Saint's use of Biblical history. For further information he consulted Maurice.

The Master was delighted. The historical novel was a *genre* in which Kingsley could accomplish the greatest good with the least antagonism, and Maurice gladly supplied the reading list that Kingsley had asked for. *The Life of Apollonius of Tyana* by Philostratus, provided some idea of the effort to combine 'miracle-working and a semi-divine person with philosophy'. Philo, Maurice thought, would show him the Jewish origin of that effort, while Clemens would explain it in its highest Christian form; and for a concrete example of sect warfare resembling that in contemporary England, Maurice recommended, in addition to the Alexandrian Fathers, 'the noble little book of Athanasius against the Gentiles'.[5]

While Maurice was quietly editing *Yeast* for Parker's, Kingsley was steeping himself in history. He read assiduously, and in mid-October he reported that Hypatia was 'growing', and that he was 'getting very fond of her'. The period was dark and the people often unethical but there were nevertheless materials for a fine book.[6]

The story was serialized monthly in *Fraser's Magazine*. It began in January, 1852 and, except for the November and December single-chapter submissions, it continued in two-chapter instalments until April, 1853. In each of these the first chapter generally taught the lesson, while the second offered an episode of turbulent action and excitement. After the appearance of the sixth instalment, Kingsley paused to reflect and decided to insert a piece for his readers. Dropping his authorial mask, he addressed them directly in an explanatory interpolation, which was to become the Preface in the book. This Preface, then, sketches the history of the period and indicates Maurice's view that history was a reconciling process between opposing elements in society and, in this case, not only between a corrupt eastern and a healthier western Christianity, but also between a southern Latin polity and that of the Gothic north; and while readers can enjoy the story without a knowledge of Kingsley's deeper purposes, an awareness of them invests his novel with the epic view of history that he and Maurice considered vital for social reform in their own society.

Ample in scope and conception, *Hypatia* concentrates on the second decade of the fifth century. 'Born into the world almost at the same moment', the Roman Empire and the Christian church had been rivals for four hundred years, each engaged against the other 'in a deadly struggle for the possession of the human race'. But now the Goths under Alaric had sacked Rome and, profiting by her debility, Alexandria had expanded and rivalled Rome herself. Here had developed a great school of Neoplatonic philosophy and, as the strongest contender for the old gods, it had become the greatest single rival of the now powerful Alexandrian or Eastern Church. Here, therefore, in 413 A.D. occurred the last struggle between paganism and Christianity, and Hypatia herself became the focal-point of the battle.

Kingsley pictures Alexandria as a welter of contending races, creeds, and political factions. In the social ferment of the time, Jews, Romans, and Greeks struggled for supremacy as troupes of Goths indifferently plundered one group or another, killing, playing, feeding and drinking, and forging their dauntless way through the throbbing multitudes as fancy dictated. Philammon, a young monk from the desert, thrilled to the metropolis, but in helping Cyril's *parabolani*[7] with district visiting among the Greek element of the city, he saw the darker side of 'the greatest seaport in the world'. Neglected 'in body, house, and soul', these Greeks, like the masses in Victorian London, lived in squalor and misery, only proving their existence from time to time by 'aimless and sanguinary riots'.[8] The old Jewess, Miriam, symbolized the corruption, for the twisted crone was always watching and waiting, fixing the great ones with an evil eye as with feigned innocence she carried letters of intrigue to one and all – but always, after she had scanned them for her own devious ends. Kingsley made brutality and fanaticism the leading features of the metropolis, which he summed up as a 'rotting and aimless chaos'.

Beneath the restless flux, however, the Christian Fathers were at work with 'a breadth of observation' enabling them to absorb the best of Greek philosophy and Roman polity into a Christian metaphysic, and Augustine (354–430) was the father ideally suited to Kingsley's purpose. Like Maurice, Augustine had regarded the family as the nucleus of society, and both agreed with Plato and St. Paul in declaring righteousness – right and just action – to be the essence of harmonious human relationships. *Justicia* demanded morality, and every act thus became a response to one of two loyalties: 'Two loves have created two cities: love of self, to the contempt of God, the earthly city; love of God, to the contempt of self, the heavenly'.[9] Thus Augustine's *City of God* spoke of an ideal society for all men and his City, like Maurice's Kingdom, was the heavenly and eternal goal beyond the ocean of time, to which all men of good will directed their actions; and *Hypatia* was to portray Englishmen 'in toga and tunic, rather than coat and bonnet'.

Hypatia's story is graphically conveyed by Toland's title-page, where she is described as beautiful and virtuous, learned and accomplished. She was 'torn to pieces' by the clergy of Alexandria to gratify the pride and cruelty of their archbishop, 'commonly but undeservedly' styled St. Cyril. Socrates' *History* names her as the daughter of the philosopher, Theon, and also emphasizes her cultivation, refinement, and beauty. It also notes that she succeeded to the school of Plato and Plotinus as the greatest philosopher of her time.

But in spite of the esteem in which she was held, she was victimized by the prevailing 'political jealousies' of the time and, owing to her frequent interviews with Orestes, the Roman Prefect in Alexandria, it was 'calumniously reported among the Christian populace' that her influence alone prevented his reconciliation with Cyril. Socrates adds that the Christians under their ringleader, Peter the Reader, were carried away by 'a fierce and bigoted zeal', and entered into 'a conspiracy against her'.

Observing her returning home in her carriage, they dragged her from it, and carried her to the church called Caesareum, where they completely stripped her, and then murdered her with shells. After tearing her body in pieces, they took her mangled limbs to a place called Cinaron, and there burnt them.[10]

These are the facts on which Kingsley based his fiction.

Kingsley's heroine possesses the mind and beauty of the Greek. Depicted as coldly intellectual, she sees a conflict, not merely between paganism and Christianity but, more especially, between the culture of an exclusive aristocracy and the sensuous Alexandrian populace. Her intellectual abstractions are as unattainable as unwanted by the 'vulgar herd', and her abhorrence of Christianity resides in its concern with these 'human and low-born' creatures.

Learning is fashionable, and in Kingsley's novel Hypatia's lectures are both renowned and popular. Like Mackaye's book-shop in *Alton Locke*, her lecture-hall is the focal-point of the story, and to it come 'philosophers and philophasters, students and fine gentlemen'. For his own devious purposes, the nominally Christian Orestes appears there, as does the evil but resilient Miriam. And largely to annoy her rival comes Pelagia, the beautiful *danseuse*, accompanied by her court of Gothic admirers while, from the peaceful brotherhood of the Laura arrives Philammon, who hopes to convert Hypatia to Christianity. And there, also, is Raphael Aben-Ezra, the rich and inscrutable Jew who, in search of God, wanders about Alexandria with Bran, his British mastiff, at his heels.

Raphael's role is not unlike that of Lancelot Smith in *Yeast*. He is handsome and 'gorgeously bedizened', but is a profligate who is bored, lazy, and contemptuous. When Cyril raises 30,000 monks and pillages the Jewish quarter, Raphael accepts the resulting exodus with indifference; and to Hypatia's pleading that he remain in Alexandria he replies that she is 'far too lovely' for his peace of mind. Though for her part she maintains a passionless front, she has recognized him as 'superior in that moral earnestness and strength of will for which she [looks] in vain among the enervated Greeks'. Her most cherished hope has been to convert him to Neoplatonism, but her philosophy has failed to hold him. Kingsley's aim, however, is to convert the Jew to Christianity, and this becomes the principal theme in the novel.

Sitting between the bare walls of a 'fire-scarred tower' in the

Roman *campagna*, Raphael, the 'new Diogenes', is attempting to solve the age-old problem – 'Given self; to find God'. But as he gazes outward to the 'purple mountains and the silver sea', his help comes, not from the hills, but from Bran.[11] The only friend he has, she demands his respect because she is always true to her dog nature.[12]

Kingsley actually presents the elementary but fundamental ethics of Christian socialism in the instinctive but responsible behaviour of the dog. When she is torn between loyalty to him and her new-born puppies, she obeys her nature and turns to her off-spring; and her spontaneous acceptance of her responsibility induces Raphael to accept his. Though at his heels in true dog fashion she none the less leads him to the rescue of a Roman General who is also a Prefect, and through a series of practical but intuitive measures suggested by her, the General, his daughter Victoria and, finally, her brother, are all rescued. Bran is an abler teacher than Hypatia,[13] for these object-lessons humanize Raphael and show him something of the nature of love.

When Maurice read the introductory instalments as they appeared in *Fraser's*, he pronounced Kingsley's handling of the tale to be 'true' and 'very powerful'. But although he was not to sacrifice 'dramatic truth' to sect and party feelings, he was not to tread unnecessarily on anyone's toes. He was, however, to delete the occasional description in order to avoid the accusations of volup-tuousness. But more importantly, since after twelve chapters he had now set up Greek and Jew 'specimens' of the expiring Alexandrian world, in addition to a strong Latin personality, he needed 'an earnest Latin [character], not of Italy, but probably [one] with a mixture of African blood'. 'Take a look at *De Civitate Dei*', Maurice advised, for 'the metaphysical parts' of that book show 'wherein the Latin character surpassed the Greek'. In that treatise Kingsley could see for himself how Augustine had put the case for 'a re-generate social order in the universe' by showing how the Latin mind had met the Gothic and combined with it, while the Greek had regarded it as merely 'uncouth'. He could also see, Maurice said, that 'the reverence for women' and the Gothic dream of domes-ticity – however alien from the conditions at the time – 'were capable of assimilating with those older parts of the Latin character which the Christian Church [had] educated and again made mighty'.[14] Maurice had it in mind that Kingsley should illustrate that 'God's world was good' and that the course of history proved it.

Kingsley therefore introduced Augustine, and in his characterization of the Saint reposes the philosophy of history that the bishop had expounded in *The City of God*, and which Maurice wanted Kingsley to illustrate in his novel. And although the delineation of the bishop's character does this, Kingsley, as we have seen, had first interpolated 'The Author to his Readers', outlining Augustine's exposition of history as unfolding in reconciling widely differing civilizations – largely, it would seem, to clarify Maurice's interpretation of Augustine in his own mind before continuing with his novel.

Kingsley's most pressing concern, however, is Raphael's conversion. How can Raphael be brought under Augustine's influence? Again, Maurice has the answer. Let either the Christian Victoria or her father persuade Raphael 'to hear one of Augustine's sermons'. Let the subject be a Psalm in which Augustine 'refines and allegorizes without mercy' so that Raphael, feeling that the bishop is treating David's Psalms as Hypatia had treated Homer, is thoroughly annoyed. The result of this is to be portrayed, Maurice suggests, as eliciting from Raphael much of the 'sound Hebrew feeling' that had been stifled by Neoplatonism.[15] And once this feeling is roused, Augustine can then reveal himself as the powerful preacher he is, and can proclaim a God of absolute Love, whom Raphael and the uncouth Africans will accept 'with an intelligence which transfigures their countenances and raises them into human beings!'[16] In short, Raphael and the soldiers are all to be converted to Christianity by Augustine's sermon, Raphael seeing that 'the God of the Creed' is the God of Abraham.

Before acting on Maurice's suggestion, however, Kingsley carefully prepares the sceptical Raphael for his meeting with Augustine. The Jew gradually grows more selfless by observing human examples of it. Victoria's only thought is for her father, while he, the General, encumbers his own escape for the sake of his wounded men. Emulating their selflessness, Raphael spends great sums in buying wheat for the party in the *campagna*, and as Augustine tells the unsuspecting philanthropist that he is 'not far from the kingdom of God', Raphael feels that sacrifice does indeed bear witness to God:

... 'since I have seen you and your daughter, and, strangest of all, your gay young Alcibiades of a son, starving yourselves to feed those poor ruffians – performing for them, day and night, the offices of menial slaves – comforting them, as no man ever comforted me – blaming no one but yourselves, caring for everyone but yourselves, sacrificing nothing but yourselves. . . . When I saw that, sir, . . . I found most unexpectedly those very grand moral rules which you were practising, . . . [and] then, sir, I began to suspect that the creed which could produce such deeds as I have watched within the last few days, might have on its side . . . what we Jews used once to call . . . the mighty power of God'.[17]

Then, after reading the Epistle to the Hebrews, he concludes that Paul knew more of Plato than all the ladies and gentlemen in Hypatia's school. In his own way, the Jew is passing through the now familiar stages of conversion.[18] *Hypatia* thus becomes a 'yeast' of the ancient world and its plot, like that of the earlier seminal novel, discloses a hero developing a sense of mission and thus turning to Christian socialism.

But Kingsley heightens the suspense with disillusionment. In love with Victoria, Raphael is on the point of becoming a Christian: 'I had actually deluded myself', he tells the Prefect, 'into the fancy that the Deity of the Galileans might be, after all, the God of our Hebrew forefathers . . . and that Paul was right – actually right – in his theory that the church was the development and fulfilment of our old national polity'.[19] But he repudiates the celibate life that the General has planned for his daughter. Celibacy, he declares as he turns away in disgust, will 'stultify the primary laws' of her nature. Romance is nipped in the bud and thus the reader is kept on tenter-hooks for another seventy pages before Kingsley can act on his mentor's suggestion.

When Raphael next appears he is with Synesius, the Squire-Bishop of Cyrene. Synesius is a very human Christian who, in the course of his chequered career, has married, loved, and lost; and Raphael feels that he can confide in him. He confesses his love for

Victoria, whom he will lose, he thinks, not because of her religion, but because her father is insisting on a fallacious interpretation of it. In his view, 'philosophers, Jews, and Christians' have all read their sacred books 'to mean anything or nothing', so that neither truth nor reason can prevail.

But at this point, just as in *Yeast*, Barnakill is introduced, so in *Hypatia*, Augustine appears with the General's party to cheer and assist the two men and, although Augustine remains the polished and learned bishop of history, he is Kingsley's instrument for the resolution of the plot. In a few bold strokes Kingsley sketches the Christian Father in whose 'mighty countenance' is 'the calm of a worn-out volcano'. Kingsley's portrait shows him as Maurice had advised. Raphael finds that

Augustine knows what evil is, ... that he has had it in him and has wrestled with it to the death. He knows it too in its palpable outward forms. He is altogether practical, and all the controversies of the schools about evil have been translated into facts and realities by his experiences. Moreover, Raphael perceives, to his wonder, that he knows *God*, ... [and] this God, in whom he is living and moving, is as personal and substantial as any Hebrew could believe Him to be, the Warrior with Evil, the Conqueror of it.[20]

Augustine is a great man because he has faced evil and has overcome it through the personal experience of God's Love. Raphael instinctively kneels for his blessing, and Synesius assures him that he will soon 'enter into the fruition of it'.[21]

Augustine's sermon also develops along the lines suggested by Maurice. It asserts 'a Living Present God' whom Augustine has discovered in his successful battle with evil. Kingsley tells it just as Maurice had advised. Raphael experiences all the appropriate changes in feeling, and in his conversion he reveals the hand of God at work in history, whether personal or national:

What if Augustine were right after all? What if the Jehovah of the old Scriptures were not merely the national patron of the children of Abraham, as the Rabbis held; not merely, as Philo held, the Divine Wisdom which inspired a few elect sages, even among the heathen; but the Lord of the whole earth, and of the nations thereof? ... What if Augustine were right in going even further than Philo and Hypatia?

What if this same Jehovah, Wisdom, Logos, call Him what they might, were actually the God of the spirits, as well as of the bodies of all flesh? What if He was as near – Augustine said that He was – to the hearts of those wild Markmen, Gauls, Thracians, as to Augustine's own heart? What if He were – Augustine said He was – yearning after, enlightening, leading home to Himself, the souls of the poorest, the most brutal, the most sinful? . . . What if He loved man as man, and not merely one favoured race or one favoured class of minds? . . . And in the light of that · hypothesis, that strange story of the Cross of Calvary seemed not so impossible after all.[22]

Maurice assumed that the fictional convert, like the real ones he knew, would have practical difficulties to discuss, and he had told Kingsley how Raphael might be dealt with. But the disciple is more artistic than the master. Once converted, Raphael goes immediately into action, and the theology that Maurice would have expounded, the intelligent Raphael is shown to know already: he who loses his life shall find it; and the City of God and the Kingdom of heaven are identical names for a state to which all men aspire. He admits 'that the Jews expected such a kingdom, and that it was not revealed till the Son of God took flesh and overcame death'. He also agrees that Hypatia and the Neoplatonists 'are dreaming, and not falsely, of such a kingdom as existing'.

In *Moral and Metaphysical Philosophy* Maurice had explained that in Christianizing Platonism the Church fathers had shown that the only 'satisfactory interpretation' of Neoplatonism reposed in Christianity. According to them, the brotherhood which the ⌐ philosophers had regarded as an exclusive fraternity of sages, was accessible to 'the poorest peasant' because it had 'pleased God to establish a communion in the person of One who was himself poor and suffering'. That communion, the Eucharist, to which all men are admitted, was indeed a mystery, but it was a very different one from the communion of the Neoplatonists. The difference between the mystery admitting men to the fraternity of Neoplatonists, and that admitting them to the inclusive Christian brotherhood was 'precisely that which Plato pointed out between the darkness of the sophist and the darkness of the "pure philosopher" '. The darkness enveloping the sophist was the cloud of his own rhetorical and logical understanding in which he concealed the light from himself. The darkness surrounding the Christian, on the other hand, came from the 'excess of light' in which he dwelt as a 'pure philosopher'. His light, though that of his imaginative reason, was a human and therefore a necessarily pale reflection of that Living Light, the Primary Imagination of the Triune Godhead.[23]

Raphael begins his mission by attempting to convert Hypatia and he starts, fittingly enough, with an explanation of the Trinity. In other words, Kingsley attempts to explain Maurice through Raphael. The invisible I AM satisfies both Raphael and the Neoplatonist. Using her own dialectic, Raphael shows Hypatia easily enough that man is the genus, the philosopher the species; that man is a person, a creature with a will and, of necessity, a son; that if Plato is accepted, there is an archetypal Man, who is also an archetypal Person, Will, and Son. Then he identifies righteousness with love, which he describes as a spirit desiring 'the highest good for man'. Unlike Neoplatonism, Christianity is not an intellectual, but a moral philosophy.

All this, Hypatia accepts. But she recoils from the thought that a crucified Son can also be a crucified God. But in archetypal terms of the father–son relationship, Raphael's argument holds good, and the sacrificial cross is seen as the only means of freeing each one of us from the suspicion of self-interest. Thinking of Victoria in the light of Augustine's sermon, Raphael has a vision, at once Christian and social:

What if I had seen a human being, a woman, too, a young weak girl, showing forth the glory and the beauty of God? Showing me that the beautiful was to mingle unshrinking, for duty's sake, with all that is most foul and loathsome; that the sublime was to stoop to the most menial offices; . . . that to be heavenly, was to know that the commonest relations, the most vulgar duties, of earth, were God's commands, and only to be performed aright by the help of the same spirit by which He rules the universe; that righteousness was to love, to help, to suffer for – if need be, to die for – those who, in themselves, seem fitted to arouse no feelings except indignation and disgust? . . . What if I, a Platonist, like John of Galilee, and Paul of Tarsus, yet, like them, a Hebrew of the Hebrews, had confessed to myself – If the creature can love thus, how much more its archetype? If weak woman can endure thus, how much more a Son of God (Ch. XVII, 347).

The preacher proclaims these principles of love and selflessness to be universal. Contemporary indifference to the masses has arisen from dreams like those of Hypatia, who has departed from Plato as nineteenth-century idealism under a spurious doctrinal christianity has forsaken the simple teaching of Jesus: sectarian system-building is Neoplatonic rather than Christian. In an attempt to make religion intellectual rather than moral, Kingsley's generation are degrading Christianity into 'a barren and lifeless phantom, a mere projection of the human brain, attributing reality to mere conceptions and names, and confusing the subject with the object'. They are doing, in fact, what the logicians declared the Neoplatonists to have done in the age of Hypatia.[24] Hypatia herself is made to tell Philammon that 'it is not enough to say, with the Christians, that God has made the world, if we make that very assertion an excuse for believing His presence to have been since withdrawn from it'.[25]

Kingsley declared *Hypatia* to be 'a strictly historical tale' based on 'the historical facts'. But the novel is surely coloured by his imagination, and his description of the philosopher's terrible end indicates man's inhumanity to man:

She shook herself free from her tormentors, and springing back, rose for one moment to her full height, naked, snow-white against the dusky mass around – shame and indignation in those wide clear eyes, but not a stain of fear. With one hand she clasped her golden locks around her; the other long white arm was stretched upward toward the great still Christ appealing – and who dare say, in vain? – from man to God. Her lips were opened to speak; but the words that should have come from them reached God's ear alone; for in an instant Peter struck her down, the dark mass closed over her again . . . and then wail on wail, long, wild, ear-piercing, rang along the vaulted roofs, and thrilled like the trumpet of avenging angels through Philammon's ears (Ch. XXIX, 362).

So evil deeds are done, sanctioned for ends which, however good in themselves, are cursed by the execrable means that foul them.

As the novel draws to a close, Peter and his vile associates remain safe in the sanctuary, thus escaping the swords of the Goths. And although Cyril 'would have given his own right hand' to have avoided the assassination, he refuses to deliver the murderers to justice since his task, he declares, is to establish 'the kingdom of

God' in Alexandria. In one bold stroke Kingsley relays several aspects of Maurice's teaching, the most important of which are the authenticity of the conscience and the continuing tendency to replace a divinely sanctioned social scheme with systems devised by egotheists:

> In the hour of that unrighteous victory, the Church of Alexandria received a deadly wound. It had admitted and sanctioned those habits of doing evil that good may come, of pious intrigue, and at last of open persecution, which are certain to creep in wheresoever men attempt to set up a merely religious empire, independent of human relationships and civil laws; – to 'establish', in short, a 'theocracy', and by that very act confess their secret disbelief that God is ruling already (Ch. xxx, 381).

Cyril and his monks are inhabitants of Augustine's earthly city, which thrives within the church itself:

> Bishops kissing the feet of parricides and harlots. Saints tearing saints in pieces for a word, while sinners cheer them on to the unnatural fight. Liars thanked for lying, hypocrites taking pride in their hypocrisy. The many sold and butchered for the malice, the caprice, the vanity of the few. The plunderers of the poor plundered in their turn by worse devourers than themselves.[26]

How changeless the world, whether Byzantium or Alexandria, Rome or London!

But *Hypatia* is not lacking in nobler characters revealing other relationships. Amal the Amalric, god-like and golden-haired, is acclaimed by all as he comes forward. Accompanied everywhere by forty barbarians and their attendant mistresses, including his own Pelagia, he boasts descent from Odin. He is the hero of the Goths, 'their heavenly man', their joy and pride, who 'belonged to them, bone of their bone, flesh of their flesh' (Ch. xix, 368).

But he is less heroic than he seems. In 'The Bower of Acrasia' (Ch. xii) he is a veritable Verdant and Bacchus combined, his 'mighty limbs stretched out on cushions, his yellow hair crowned with vine leaves, his hand grasping a golden cup'. Despite his physique he is unmanly and morally weak. He wastes his potential for leadership and abandons himself to wantonness. When worsted by Philammon in their struggle over Pelagia, he fails his adoring

Goths, who regard his untimely death as Odin's just punishment for his intemperance.

The Kingsleian hero is above all a man of moral strength, and Raphael turns from Hypatia's philosophy in search of *a man*. At the close of the novel that man is found to be the 'crucified one' – Plato's 'righteous man' – whose veracity even Hypatia cannot deny.[27] He personifies disinterestedness, which for Kingsley epitomizes moral strength, and which Raphael believes to emanate from the Spirit of God. Like Philammon, Raphael sees that the genuine hero is 'a man in the image of God', not physically, of course, since God is a Spirit, but morally. He knows his strength, not as his own, but as God's.

Slothful though the Amal is, Kingsley never allows the reader to forget his noble potential. It matches his splendid physique and in spite of his casual behaviour the Amal is heroic as Hypatia and Cyril are not. Hypatia is virtuous and she dies heroically. Cyril is a successful schemer, while Orestes is astute and ingratiating. But none of them is interested in the populace that each is seeking to control. Because the Amal loves his barbarians he is closer to 'that crucified one' than they, and correspondingly more heroic.

Further insight into Kingsley's characterizations is provided by a comparison of the three principal female characters in the book. As Hypatia symbolizes intellectual virtue, Pelagia represents concupiscence, and Victoria becomes the mean between them. It is significant for Kingsley's marriage thesis that as Raphael moves toward Christianity simultaneously as Hypatia recedes from it, he falls in love with a virtuous but flesh-and-blood woman. Like Arthur in the *Faerie Queene*, Victoria is identified with Magnificence, which Spenser classified with Christian 'perseverence'.[28]

While history makes its own contribution to the kind of character drawn, the female portraits provide examples of fictional characterization brought to the aid of history. Kingsley, however, was driven beyond mere character reconciliation as represented in Victoria. In order to comply with Maurice's request he has to show character in the historical process itself. He has to transfer the 'identity in opposites' from individuals to society and to maintain a parallel between men and movements. Historical action must show a reconciling action between good and evil, between the City and the world, and the meaning of history must be demonstrated in character itself. This is the ultimate significance both of Raphael and Augustine.

Doing double duty as an historical figure and a fictional character, Augustine is made the unifying centre in the novel. He establishes Christianity as the predominant mode of society just then taking shape, and he does so by going to the cardinal theme of Christianity – righteousness, or right action. The Bishop is a great man making history, and the versatile Kingsley does his best with a theme that is obviously congenial. But instead of emphasizing Augustine's centrality in a climactic meeting with Raphael and thus fixing the epical process of historical becoming on Augustine, he embodies it only in soliloquy as Raphael weighs the effect of the Bishop's sermon on the rough soldiers.

. . . whether or not Augustine knew truths for all men, he at least knew sins for all men, and for himself as well as his hearers. . . . What he rebuked in others, he had felt in himself, and fought it to the death-grip, as the flash and quiver of that worn face proclaimed.

Sin, Raphael sees, comes from within and it can never be conquered in the world until it has been conquered within:

Could the legionaries permanently put down the lust and greed around them, while their own hearts were enslaved to lust and greed within? . . . Could they restore unity and peace to the country while there was neither unity nor peace within them? What had produced the helplessness of the people, . . . but inward helplessness, inward weakness (Ch. xxi, 271)?

The fictional Augustine speaks to fictional characters to make them and Kingsley's readers look within in order to take appropriate action. The historical Christian father directs mankind in all ages to do likewise and strongly to will right action for progressive history that will lead them toward the City.

Raphael's characterization is equally significant, and in departing from Maurice's advice Kingsley both lost and gained. Since Raphael's interview with the Bishop follows his sermon and Raphael's soliloquy on it, something of an anticlimax is the result. But more importantly, the historical reconciliation is weakened, and the import of history is correspondingly muted. On the other hand, Raphael needed Kingsley's attention more than Augustine who, after all, has the advantage of being a historical personage. Judaism and Christianity meet, but by soliloquizing on the preacher's effect on the soldiers, the Jew retains something of his Jewishness while at the same time extending Augustine's sphere of influence. Kingsley thus makes Raphael a more powerful character. As a Jew, he embodies Scripture. But he also indicates abandoned Neoplatonism, for it has failed him in his hour of need. Now, he not only accepts Augustine's sermon, but he extends it to the soldiers, and so to the national society they represent. The fictional embodiment of Judaism and the Augustinian theology that has supplanted his discarded Neoplatonism, Raphael represents the 'heirloom' bequeathed by a dying civilization to a new.

Structure, theme, and character-portrayal are thus seen to merge in Raphael's conversion, itself freighted, both with a personal change of heart and the meaning of history. Raphael emerges from the mists of antiquity into the turbulence of Alexandria and, in unobtrusively bringing Hypatia to a vision of the faith, he is stamped with the wisdom of Christ and remains inevitably compelling. His growth in personal clarity is coincident with the growth of the novel itself, and his final portrait is one of calm conviction and imperturbable strength. He is history itself. We need 'Hebrew men', Kingsley told a Jewish student who liked *Hypatia*, 'to teach us the real meaning of the Old Testament, and its absolute unity with the New'[29] and, modelled as he is on Kingsley's friend, a Jewish lawyer and convert, Alfred Hyman Louis, Raphael is such a man.[30] A vital mouthpiece for several themes the most important of which is enlightened social Christianity, he has undergone a laudable metamorphosis from Lancelot Smith to become Kingsley's most memorable character.

Almost insurmountable difficulties shadowed Kingsley in *Hypatia* and the fact that so few of his critics recognized the nature of them indicates the extent of his skill in handling them. *Hypatia* is one of those odd novels in which the heroine, dying, must be presented with sufficient detachment to make her death acceptable, and

Kingsley consistently maintains a delicate balance in Hypatia's portrait. Intellectual coldness, inhumanity, and a stubborn adherence to her theories oppose virtue, beauty, and grace in achieving a subtle but ultimately unsympathetic figure. When her death-wails have died away and the dreadful scene has drawn to a close, the reader's feeling is one of pent-up relief. The air has been cleared and the whole community purged.

Two other factors hampered the artistic treatment and endangered the narrative. According to history, Hypatia is murdered by the Christians. It also makes scoundrels of Peter and Cyril. Kingsley however, contrived to tell his story and to impart their distorted vision without alienating his readers from Christianity itself. On the other hand, history fails to record the just nemesis deeply desired for both but, though deferred in the novel, their punishment brings a measure of satisfaction, and the visitation of their sins upon the whole church strengthens the lesson in Christian socialism. Kingsley sustained a delicate balance between individuals and society, between men and movements.

But in Augustinian terms Alexandria is a world in which good and evil co-exist. Dwellers in the City necessarily intermingle with those in the world since, although Augustine described the two cities as being incompatible, they co-exist simultaneously, as we have seen, and consequently find a *modus vivendi*. While never really mingling they live side by side in a manner allowing the City, not only to grow but, in the fullness of time, to absorb the world. 'On earth,

the celestial society increases itself out of all languages, being unconcerned by the different temporal laws that are made; yet not breaking but observing their diversity in divers nations, so long as they tend unto the preservation of earthly peace, and do not oppose the adoration of one God alone. . . . This peace is that unto which the pilgrim in faith refers the other peace, which he has here in his pilgrimage; and then lives he according to the faith, when all that he does for the obtaining thereof is by himself referred unto God, and his neighbour withal, because, being a citizen, he must not be all for himself, but sociable in his life and actions.[31]

Hypatia imparts this double vision.

Co-existence means a reconciliation of likenesses in opposites, and Kingsley kept this concept steadily in view as he worked his way forward. Representing both elements in Jewish polity, the 'evil-eyed' Miriam and the truth-seeking Raphael are mother and son. In their eventual reconciliation Miriam gives way to Raphael who, though a profligate when the story opens, gradually eschews her evil schemes and her superstition in his search for God. The struggle continues in Hypatia and Raphael. In the course of time and in the process of history Hypatia and the classical paganism that she represents, recede as ancient and irrefutable truth represented by Raphael proceeds westward in search of faith. Meanwhile, good and evil co-exist in the Roman west, and as the union of Victoria and Raphael accomplishes the desired east–west synthesis, so Maurice's 'earnest Latin [character] with a mixture of African blood' accomplishes the north–south, Gothic–Roman fusion. The heirloom that Kingsley and the Christian socialists are determined to preserve in England culminates in the coalescence of all these strands of civilization.

Has history achieved its goal, then, with the establishment of Christianity? Even here, Maurice supplied the answer. Augustine had evolved a philosophy of history, for he had seen the permanence behind the flux. 'But oh! beware, Augustine, that a new tyranny, more detestable and accursed, does not spring out of its ruins; a tyranny built upon the attempt to set up a kingdom of Heaven on earth in the name of Christ, on the denial that Christ has set it up already'.[32] Though Neoplatonism has been crushed, Cyril's church is transforming itself into a Papacy and in due course Luther and Calvin are to counter a city on the seven hills of Rome, allegedly eternal. System-building is the snare, and the golden mean must ever be kept in view as mankind travel onward toward the City.

As Kingsley was writing *Hypatia*, Maurice was preparing his *Theological Essays* (1853)[33] in which, in addition to that on eternal punishment, he included one on the nature of sin. In adopting the name Pelagia, Kingsley deliberately drew attention to Pelagius (*c* 360–*c*. 420), who had denied the doctrine of original sin. The British-born theologian had seriously divided the Church for more than a decade before he was declared heretical. Neither Maurice nor

Kingsley denied original sin, but they felt that the subject, like that of eternal punishment, badly needed re-thinking.

Kingsley's Pelagia personifies sin though, as a pagan, 'right and wrong [are] ideas unknown to her. . . .' As the Amal's mistress, she also represents concupiscence. She plays Aphrodite in stark nakedness before Orestes, Hypatia, and the assembled Alexandrian throng; and Philammon, who has just discovered that she is his sister, is overcome with remorse. Her redemption becomes his sole object.

As the gravity of her situation dawns upon her, Pelagia is distraught. Prince Wulf has transferred his favour to Hypatia, who 'has no gospel for the harlot'. Philammon had hoped that penance might save her but, when she recalls her baptism, even he her brother thinks she must perish. Indeed, since his feelings are supported by the old monk, Arcanius, God Himself despises her, it seems. Punishment is to be hers for eternity. She cries out in anguish:

The flames of hell for ever! Oh, not for ever! Great, dreadful God! Not for ever! . . . Thou wilt not send me to burn for ever and ever? . . . Will not a hundred years be punishment enough – or a thousand (Ch. xxviii, 358)?

Like Pelagia, Raphael is also grappling with evil. Pelagia, he knows, is loved and loving. She is a creature of great good will. She has saved Philammon's life and is ready to die for the Amal if by so doing she can restore him to the throne of the Ptolemies, where he belongs. If she is to be punished for eternity, then none can be saved, Raphael decides, and least of all, himself. Had he not encouraged Hypatia's alliance with Orestes, thus supporting, even urging her contention against the Christians? 'He, not Peter, was the murderer of Hypatia!' Her death lay at his door and he, Raphael, was a sinner and a murderer – a man obsessed by evil. At one with Pelagia in his sin, at one with Augustine in his struggle with evil, Raphael learns at last the nature of God's love.

Man's sin lies in his pretention to goodness in himself. For all his anti-Pelagianism, Augustine proclaimed again and again the Spirit of Love and God's 'absolute good will'. In the Spirit of

Christ, Raphael can only cast himself upon God: what benediction, what peace, to know at last that He returns 'good for evil'. 'Given self; to find God' may be the problem of philosophy, but to hear His voice is to walk *secundum Deum* in the way of love, and this is the path of the Christian.[34] As brother and sister, Philammon and Pelagia share the Eucharist in the desert before their translation to the City of God.

CHAPTER 6

Westward Ho!

Kingsley wrote *Westward Ho!* when he was on leave in Devon
absorbing the charm of his native hills and, for the first time since
his marriage, enjoying the seashore with his children. As Mrs.
Kingsley's health improved in the sunny warmth of Torquay the
spirits of the family rose and, since Kingsley had leisure for reading,
Froude, who lived close by at Babbacombe and was working on
his *History of England*,[1] lured him into Elizabethan literature, so
that *Westward Ho!* became his second historical novel.

Expeditions to Torbay gave rise to a journal, and *Glaucus*,
which grew out of it, includes the germ of *Westward Ho!* Meditating
on the bay's 'blue ring of water', Kingsley wrote of the 'glow'
that came over him whenever he recalled

the terrible and glorious pageant which passed by in the glorious July
days of 1588, when the Spanish Armada ventured slowly past Berry
Head, with Elizabeth's gallant pack of Devon captains . . . following
fast in its wake, and dashing into the midst of the vast line, undismayed
by size and numbers, . . .[2]

That 'blue ring' bounded by 'great limestone bluffs' suddenly
became the setting of the play enacted there three hundred years
before, when his Elizabethan forebears had played their part with
courage and conviction as they ushered in a new age. 'The triumphal
peal of the Reformed faith' had rung across the world,[3] which then
experienced 'a sea change/Into something new and strange':

. . . from all Europe, from all of mankind . . . in which lay the seed of
future virtue and greatness, . . . and the triumphs of the coming age of
science, arose a shout of holy joy, such as the world had not heard for
many a weary and bloody century; a shout which was the prophetic
birth-paean of North America, Australia, New Zealand, the Pacific
Islands, of free commerce and free colonization over the whole earth
(Ch. XXXII, 569).

The past had coincided with the present, and as Kingsley gazed on the scene that had witnessed the gathering of Spanish ships for the destruction of England, there flashed upon his mind 'a web of imaginative construction'.[4] The facts had been provided by historians as unlike as Froude and Camden and as he wrote his novel he would interpret them for himself. But for this moment of dazzling imaginative truth, he saw the whole, not as historical data, but as a drama of cosmic import.

Kingsley had to write *Westward Ho!*, for having depicted the triumph of Christianity in *Hypatia* he saw that if British history, as Maurice had suggested,[5] had begun with Christianity itself, then the battle that ended the struggle between opposing principles within it in 1588 was one of the great moments in history. The story was already legendary, and this second crisis in Christian history was the logical sequel to *Hypatia*. He turned from Alexandria to the struggle between Catholics and Protestants, which, although it had begun with Martin Luther in Germany, had ended in England and the overthrow of Spain.

The political history of Christianity had only begun with the death of Hypatia, and in the passing of her age Maurice had indicated a danger inherent in the interpretation of Augustine. The Christian polity succeeding the Alexandrian church had gradually stiffened into a system during the Middle Ages, and churchmen, absorbed with power, had grown unmindful of their earthly pilgrimage as necessarily *secundum Deum*. Popes in Rome were but Alexandrian Cyrils, and in the intervening millenial age the historical process had revealed Papal Courts directed more by the city of man than the City of God, thus making the Protestant Reformation an inevitable counter-balance.

The Elizabethans had held a Providential theory of history, regarding events as 'cosmic in scope and advancing along a linear path *sub specie aeternitatis*'.[6] Spenser had advanced the theory in *The Faerie Queene*, and in his Preface to *The History of the World* (1614) Raleigh had also asserted 'God's total control of historical events'. England was God's favoured nation, His chosen instrument for the overthrow of 'bloudie and cruell' Spain, and this Providential concept had lingered on in England after it was questioned on the Continent. Maurice and Kingsley adopted it, and Kingsley planned

to make the most of it in his recommendation of the Elizabethan
period as a challenging model for his own.

Like the sixteenth, the nineteenth century was one of religious
ferment. The English Catholics were 'emancipated' in 1829, and
Tract Ninety was answered with the cry of Popery. In 1850 'the
Pope announced that he was establishing a Roman Catholic hierarchy in England', and Dr. Wiseman, the new Archbishop of
Westminster, 'issued an imprudent "pastoral" in which he referred
to His Holiness' "noble act of Apostolic authority" '. Before the
year had ended the cry of 'no Popery' had swollen to a chorus
throughout the land as Catholic–Protestant rivalry resembling that
in Elizabethan England revived in 'one massive popular outburst'.[7]

But Kingsley had a second and more cogent reason for writing
Westward Ho!. On 28 March, 1854, the Crimean war began,[8]
and in alliance with France, Britain supported Turkey against
Russia. Kingsley felt that it would have a sobering effect on the
country and even the British reversals at Alma proved, he argued,
that the 'ancient spirit' of English tenacity was not dead. He longed
to be there, but since this was impossible and he could think of
nothing else he decided to fight again with his pen.

He was diverted during the early months of 1854, however.
In February he delivered four lectures on Alexandria and her schools
at the Philosophical Institute in Edinburgh.[9] Returning from the
north he paused in London to see Maurice and others, then went
down to Eversley. On 25 March he was in Torquay before returning
to London to give evidence in the House of Commons on sanitary
conditions, and to recommend higher pay for Parish Medical
Officers; but the period of gestation was important for his novel.

A 'most ruthless bloodthirsty book' it was just what the times
needed for it was intended to show the meaning of brotherhood
and heroism. His motto for it was a paraphrase from Demosthenes,[10]
suggesting that if each soldier would but consider the manner
in which his Elizabethan forbears had come forward from every
rank and station to meet the Armada as one indivisible strength,
each would fight worthily.

But he grew increasingly uneasy about the conduct of the war.
Miss Nightingale insisted that justice was being defeated by power,

and it was later established that 'a number of senior officers' had been 'negligent, indifferent, and inefficient'[11] so that the activities during the winter of 1854–5 became a serious indictment of government. When the cholera descended like a scourge, it seemed a retributive warning that 'the day of the Lord' was indeed at hand.

The whole thing 'stunned' him, to the great detriment of his book. Unlike Tennyson, he could not write poetry about so terrible an incident as the decimation of the Light Brigade. Dwelling on the horror of it, he felt as each of those hapless six hundred must have felt in that frightful moment when

> Storm'd at with shot and shell,
> Boldly they rode and well,
> Into the jaws of Death,
> Into the mouth of Hell. . . .

Although Tennyson, like Lord Cardigan,[12] might know what he ought to do to encourage his countrymen, he was certainly 'no Tyrtaeus'.[13] His theme eulogized the Brigade, but it failed to expose the hollowness behind their misconceived heroism.

For his part, Kingsley wrote 'Brave Words for Brave Soldiers' and sent it anonymously to the theatre of war to lift the morale of the troops. It struck a frankly religious note and although *Westward Ho!* also did this it was additionally a patriotic call for Englishmen to continue their imperial expansion.[14] The Crimean war and the cholera, then, lurk beneath the surface of *Westward Ho!* and Kingsley's contemporaries were no more unmindful of these facts than of the Catholic question at home.

Kingsley wrote *Westward Ho!* by the light of 'dear old Hakluyt'. *The Principal Navigations* (1589) was his main source, and he appears to have used the second edition in three volumes. The account of the victory over the Armada, for example, is taken from Hakluyt's translation from the Latin of Emmanuel Van Meteran's history of the Low Countries.[15] He also gleaned information from the Hakluyt Society Papers. Remembering that it had been written under 'the eye of James I', he also consulted Camden's *Annals of Elizabeth*, the first part in the original Latin covering the field down to 1588, and published in 1615.[16] His 'old Elizabethan books' included

Purchas His Pilgrimes (1625), John Fox's *Book of Martyrs* (1563), Thomas Fuller's *History of the Worthies of England* (1662), and Prince's *Worthies of Devon*, while Parsons' *Leicester's Commonwealth* gave him a 'specimen' of Jesuitical 'rascality'.[17] He also referred to Raleigh's *Discovery of Guiana* (1596), using the current Schomburgh edition that he had reviewed, as well as Prescott's *Conquest of Peru* (1847); and he had probably read Froude's notes for lectures delivered at Oxford and published in 1895 as *English Seamen of the Sixteenth Century*.

Steeped in the imaginative literature of the period as well, Kingsley was not unmindful of the fact that Sir Thomas More had lectured on the philosophy of history in Augustine's *City of God*, and had thus acquainted the rising generation of young Elizabethans with the saint's Providential theory. Puttenham's *Art of English Poetry* is mentioned in the novel, while Sidney's *Arcadia* and Lyly's *Euphues* yielded information on the nature of friendship. But Spenser's *Faerie Queene* was the greatest influence, and with these authors at hand in his maritime world, Kingsley found it impossible not to people the 'little white town' of Bideford and the West Country with those redoubtable Elizabethans who, once he had begun to write, came alive and throve round him, pursuing their commercial, military, and political enterprises with the exuberance of their time.

Local tradition ascribes the title of Kingsley's novel to his friend, Dr. Henry Ackland, whose son, Charles Kingsley Ackland, was Kingsley's godson. Meeting Henry one day, 'Whither away?' asked Kingsley. 'Oh, westward-ho!' replied the doctor, waving his hand towards what was then Northam Burrows: whence the name of both the book and the place, the latter reputedly christened in honour of the book.[18] On a more literary level, Kingsley may have borrowed it from the comedy of Dekker and Webster, *West-Ward Hoe* (1607); or from Shakespeare's *Twelfth Night*.[19] The sub-title indicates the episodic nature of the book, but *westward-ho!* with its exclamation mark succinctly conveys the romance, adventure, and jaunty optimism that characterized the age.

The first edition came out in three volumes, the first of which concluded with Chapter VIII. In this volume, Kingsley announced his subject and compared Britain's heroic age with that of ancient Greece. Amyas Leigh, his rugged school-boy hero among John Oxenham's sailors on Bideford quay, is 'all alive for any sea news', and the volume details Oxenham's 'true and tragical history'. Related by the regenerate Puritan Anabaptist, Salvation Yeo, to Sir Richard Grenville, also a Puritan, and to Amyas Leigh, his Protestant godson, the history establishes the point of view for the entire novel. Yeo's tale also introduces the 'little maid' story as well as a survey of his experiences with the Inquisition. The nature of contemporary Jesuitry in England is depicted, also from a Puritan point of view, and the volume closes with an account of 'the noble brotherhood of the Rose', with its Christian social overtones.

The second volume (Ch. IX–XX, 1880 edition) unfolds further adventures to Barbadoes, Margarita, La Guayra, and elsewhere, but much of the scene in this volume is laid in Ireland, where Eustace Leigh, Amyas's 'Romish' cousin, is working for the Catholic cause. He buries the body of the Pope's Legate shortly after Amyas and Yeo have identified it as that of Nicholas Saunders, and have taken incriminating papers, including an epistle from the Pope inciting the Irish nobility against the 'illegitimate' Elizabeth. Catholic action is more fully elaborated when Italian and Spanish insurgents join the Irish at Smerwick, where Amyas captures the Spanish nobleman, Don Guzman Maria Magdalena de Soto, who meets and falls in love with Rose Salterne. Kingsley thus unites the religious and the love themes, and both of these with adventure, when the ransomed Don departs to take up his Governorship in Caracas, taking Rose with him.

Their chivalric oath to the brotherhood obliges Amyas and Frank to follow. Their exploits in the good ship *Rose* are set forth in detail, the climactic one being their concerted attack (Ch. XIX) on the Governor's house, where they learn that Rose, although happily married to the Don and still a Protestant, is living under the shadow of Eustace and the Inquisition. Discovered, attacked, and pursued by the Governor's people, the Leigh brothers retreat, stones whirling about their heads and, reaching the ship, the unconscious Amyas is pulled aboard as the wounded Frank slips from his shoulders and disappears.

Adapting a passage from Camden's account of the 1588 conflict, Kingsley describes the *Rose* in combat with the largest of three Spanish ships. 'Spanish Bloodhounds and English Mastiffs' (Ch. xx) is a patriotic digression on the superiority of English corporate action over Spanish, by which their forces are divided, and their freedom hampered. Although contrived, the account also allows Amyas to avenge the loss of his brother, and gives Kingsley an opportunity to strengthen and unify his plot as Amyas frees Hawkins's Devon men from the hold of the Spanish ship. The volume closes on a Crimean note when Amyas's men go 'down with raging fever' because the battered *Rose* has sailed inshore to carry out repairs, only to find herself in a tropical cove steaming with the pestilence.

As the third volume opens (Ch. xxi–xxxiii) they are seeking purer air on the higher ground, and having burnt the *Rose*, they build a stockade and there recuperate. Further adventures occur in the search for the golden city of Manoa, in the capture of the gold-train on the road between Santa Fé and Magdalena, and in the seizure of the Spanish galleon with its stores of treasure and precious information. Frank and Rose are lost to the Inquisition and Eustace, who has betrayed them, disappears ignominiously from the story. The 'little maid' becomes Ayacanora, goes to England and, at last, is seen as the wife of Amyas.

This is a volume of climaxes. The capture of the magnificent galleon, *The City of the True Cross*, ends the suspense in a number of themes. The White Witch, Lucy Passmore, who had accompanied Rose to La Guayra as her serving woman, is discovered below decks and tells how Frank and Rose had been burned together at the stake. The Bishop of Carthagena is found on board also, and having been instrumental in their torture, he is hanged on the spot. The final climax is the defeat of the Armada, alleged by the Spanish to have been invincible.

In the background move the historical personages. There towers Queen Elizabeth surrounded by her admiring court: the faithful Lord Burleigh, Sidney, and Raleigh with others like Spenser, serving abroad. Still more remote and shrouded, yet looming like sinister shadows, are Mary, Philip of Spain, the Duke of Parma,

and the French House of Guise. Also associated with the Queen
and binding the ends of earth to her court are the gentlemen
adventurers: Drake, knighted on 4 April, 1581, after his voyage
round the world, Sir Richard Grenville, Oxenham, Hawkins,
Raleigh, and Gilbert. Among them all and transmuting their
thoughts and feelings for the reader are the fictitious characters,
who carry on the action and give immediacy to the tale: the Leigh
brothers together with their saintly mother and their traitorous
cousin, Eustace; Salvation Yeo, Will Cary of Clovelly, Rose
Salterne and her father the Mayor of Bideford; and uniting all of
them, like Amyas himself, the Spanish Don Guzman, a noble
parallel for his liege lord, King Philip of Spain.

A simple village sermon discloses the manner in which Kingsley
expanded *Westward Ho!*. Dilating on the Assyrians' invasion of
Israel (2 Kings, xix, 15–19), he declared history to show nations
at their best and most courageous in times of danger, when they
become greater than themselves and, with the help of their heroes,
accomplish deeds that bring glory and honour. So it had been with
the English, said Kingsley, when the world had seemed against
them because they had stood up 'for the Gospel and the Bible
against the Pope of Rome'.

Defining the issue for his congregation, Kingsley averred the
King of Spain to have sent the Armada to subdue England, while
Europe had looked on, expecting to see Englishmen 'devoured',
their 'laws and liberties' denied, 'the Popish Inquisition set up, . . .
and England made a Spanish province'. But danger had stimulated
faith and courage and, instead, Europe had actually seen the people
of England

rising as one man, to fight for themselves on earth, while the tempests
of God fought for them from heaven; and all that mighty fleet of the
King of Spain routed and scattered. . . .[20]

Alight with patriotism, the sermon doubtless appealed to his un-
lettered villagers. But even as he spoke, their thoughts strayed to
brothers and friends far away in the Crimea.

But the sermon in *Westward Ho!* strikes home with greater
force. On the eve of the threatened invasion Grenville suddenly

appears in Bideford and, making his way to Burrough, is warmly welcomed by Amyas and his mother. 'What news from Court?', they ask, and are happily reassured that both Queen and country have anticipated Philip and his awesome fleet. A dauntless knight whose enthusiasm has carried the day, Sir Richard tells Amyas and Mrs. Leigh, as he has already told the Queen: 'Not England alone, but the world, the Bible, the Gospel itself [are] at stake' (Ch. xxix, 525), and England is ready.

Identical with the words expressed in his sermon, but announced by the knight, who has just come from Court, they convey a sense of national unity. In the commentary relative to the passage, Kingsley eulogizes the Elizabethan age to the disparagement of the Victorian:

Well it was for England then that her Tudor sovereigns had compelled every man (though they kept no standing army) to be a trained soldier. Well it was that Elizabeth, even in those dangerous days of intrigue and rebellion, had trusted her people enough, not only to leave them their weapons, but (what we, forsooth, in these more 'free' and 'liberal' days dare not do) to teach them how to use them. Well it was, that by careful legislation for the comfort and employment of 'the masses' (term then, thank God, unknown), she had both won their hearts, and kept their bodies in fighting order. . . . Well for England, in a word, that Elizabeth had pursued . . . a very different course from that which we have been pursuing. . . .

Then, he makes politics dependent upon morality, and criticizes the war in the Crimea:

It is the fashion now to call [Elizabeth] a despot: but unless every monarch is to be branded with that epithet whose power is not as circumscribed as Queen Victoria's is now, we ought rather to call her the most popular sovereign, obeyed of their own free will by the freest subjects which England has ever seen; confess the Armada fight to have been as great a moral triumph as it was a political one; and (now that our late boasting is a little silenced by Crimean disasters) inquire whether we have not something to learn from those old Tudor times (both quotations: Ch. xxix, 524–5).

In rendering the adventures of Amyas Leigh into modern English Kingsley created an historical novel among the best of its kind and gave his sermon the universal appeal that turned his village con- gregation into the English-speaking world.

Although Kingsley's historicism is not the main interest in this study of social Christianity in his novels, it may be said that critics prior to the First World War had begun to appreciate his use of history in fiction. Introducing a fresh edition in 1907, the editor[21] found *Westward Ho!* 'so definitely historical, so interwoven . . . with actual historical events and persons', that he traced the chronology 'of real occurrences with which the fictitious Amyas is associated'; and in 'The Historical Basis of Kingsley's *Westward Ho!*' R. Pearse Chope traces each of the major events in the novel to the source he used.[22] And in a letter of 26 November, 1855, Kingsley avowed that he neither 'asserted' nor 'denied' anything in *Westward Ho!* that he could not substantiate with 'chapter and verse . . . even to the niceties and details'.[23] He had tried, he said, 'to draw each thing either as it did happen or as it would have happened, if it had taken place in that day' and, despite occasional lapses, he succeeded very well. He also deliberately refrained from bringing Queen Elizabeth on the scene 'because she was too important a personage for [him] to attribute fictitious acts to', and his conscience smote him, he admitted, for 'that little second-hand report of her talk with Frank Leigh' (Ch. XVI, 308).

His use of history may be seen in his reply to the Barnstaple quibbler, who questioned whether Bideford had indeed 'sent more vessels to the northern trade than any other ports save Topsham and London'. The statement, Kingsley assured him, was 'a *bona fide* quotation', but significantly, he added, 'Heaven knows if it be *true*; for what is true in history?'[24] He was keenly aware of the questionable nature of data, which must always be interpreted by the historian. Although he would scarcely have gone the whole way with Collingwood[25] that there are, properly speaking, neither authorities nor data, he believed that the latter, such as they were, had been, if not 'constructed', at least modified, by the '*a priori* imagination' of the writer. Kingsley uses history rather as a detective tests inferences and indications in a modern thriller, from which he 'constructs an imaginary picture of how the crime was committed, and by whom'. But unlike the author of the detective story whose theory is always convincingly proved by the confession of the criminal, the historian has no means of verifying his own conclusions. In Kingsley's view, however, the historical novelist is on safest ground when he adheres to received data, and trusts to his imagination for the rest.

The vexed question of Kingsley's unfairness to Roman Catholics has already been adumbrated, and however justifiable the accusation with regard to other novels, it is hardly true in this. *Westward Ho!* teems with defamatory remarks about Roman Catholics. They are accused of casuistry and vilified as liars and schemers, but theological polemic is not Kingsley's concern in this novel.[26] The circumstances in which he wrote it were such as to enable him to rise above personal animosity. But in *Westward Ho!* he could no more escape the 'theological atmosphere' that Ellis Roberts deplored in a *Bookman* article on the centenary of Kingsley's birth than he could ignore the spirit of adventure that characterized the age. Both belong to it and both are essential to a faithful delineation of it. Moreover, Kingsley's sources as well as numerous modern writers who have researched the history of the period confirm his interpretation, and inadequate indeed would be the work that failed to capture both for the 'atmosphere' of the time.[27]

Like the period in which he set his novel, Kingsley was less opposed to Roman Catholicism than to that which had come to represent it: Jesuitry and the Spanish Inquisition. These were the horrors of the age, universally hated and feared. As Kingsley saw the working-class through the mind of a Chartist tailor in *Alton Locke*, so with equally vivid verisimilitude he saw the contemporary Catholic through the mind of the Jesuit. To have drawn Eustace Leigh and his accomplices, Morgan Evans and Evan Morgans (Father Parsons and Father Campion, Jesuits) in any other light would have been to falsify English history. The Society of Jesus had been founded in Paris in 1534 by Ignatius Loyola who had made the military ideal a justification for demanding 'blind' obedience in his followers, and when they had placed themselves at the disposal of the Holy See and been approved as a religious Order on 27 September, 1540, their first aim was the suppression of Protestantism.[28] In addition to establishing missions on the Spanish Main and elsewhere, they went to Ireland as the shortest and safest road to England. As the *Harleian Miscellany* has it,

The Pope had suffered so great a loss in his revenue by the utter separation of England from his authority, when Queen Elizabeth confirmed and established the Reformation . . . that he tried all means to take her out of the way, and working more especially with the potent King Philip of Spain, they both determined either to cut her off by private artifices, or, if these should fail, to subdue the nation by open force,

and the Jesuits had their part to play in the great scheme.[29] Reasonably, Kingsley made Eustace Leigh the villian of his fiction and in making him an Englishman and a cousin of the hero, Amyas, he gave deep poignancy to the manner in which family rose against family.

The plot of *Westward Ho!* is episodic. A glance at almost any chapter reveals an essay-like completeness, but the narrative quality of 'How Bideford Bridge Dined at Annery House', for example, does much more than tell that simple story. In presenting an episode, Kingsley never loses an opportunity to interweave numerous themes and to connect them with Devon and the Queen.

In *Westward Ho!* the plot circles outward in idea from that fixed and changeless centre, the English crown. Queen Elizabeth towers in awful, yet womanly Majesty, the arch defender of God and the right. When the Armada is vanquished, 'a solemn festival day' is publicly proclaimed, 'praise, honour, and glory . . . rendered unto God', and medals struck. 'It came, it saw, it fled!' is of course among them, but the motto of deepest significance for Kingsley and inscribed on the obverse side of the title-page of *Westward Ho!* announces his constructional plan. *Dux foemina facti* translates freely as 'a woman guides the operation',[30] and nothing could more pointedly indicate the nature of Kingsley's plot nor more succinctly define his adulation of woman.

Round the Queen, the Court form the inner circle of Kingsley's plot; but a larger ring, also finding its fixed centre in the Crown, encloses all England. Without, falls the larger sphere of political and commercial concern embracing Spain and western Europe, including Italy and France, the Low Countries, Scotland, and Ireland. A still greater circle draws in the Indies, east and west, and extending to the blue Pacific, contains the Spanish Main.[31] Lastly, the great circle which is the *raison d'être* for Kingsley's story is that which grows with Francis Drake (and Amyas Leigh) as he girdles the globe on his voyage round it and returns at last to that still Centre, a hero, to be crowned with the accolade of knighthood.

Drake's voyage round the world was an extraordinary achievement. 'To what extent this was a privateering venture, and to what extent it was an official act of war, may be endlessly debated'.[32] Drake's patriotism and his essentially religious approach to his endeavours, however, cannot. Both are inescapable, and this is the line that Kingsley chose to re-create. An historical novelist wishing to inculcate a lesson in chivalry and team-play, he found that history helped him with an ideal situation for the requirements of his plot.

Aiming at 'immediate popularity',[33] Kingsley transferred history to fiction. Rose Salterne is neither an historical nor an important character. She is kept in the background and remains undeveloped. She is more acted upon than acting and apparently she has no compelling religious convictions. The brotherhood founded in her honour by the infatuated young men in the locality is therefore highly improbable. But she and the brotherhood are both of the utmost importance in the structural plan of the novel, for they are the vehicles of transfer.

Kingsley also plotted a fictional series of circles as parallels for those round the Queen. Elizabeth's 'right hand', Devon becomes a miniature England and, as the local belle, Rose Salterne, like Queen Elizabeth in the great world outside, is the centre of attraction. Although this secondary ring is parallel to the principal one, it is at the same time subordinate to it, and contained within it. Rose (the name suggests the 'virgin' Queen) becomes 'that peerless Oriana' for whom her local admirers would vanquish one another until it occurs to them that 'under the queen's laws' no man dare 'call his sword or his courage his own'. In the racy conversation establishing both this Elizabethan chivalry and the novel's plot Kingsley deftly slips from 'our peerless queen' to 'her gracious Majesty'; and Frank's arrival from Court to preside at the ceremony establishing the brotherhood unites both.

Coalescing parallels of this kind are a major constructional device. As the hero of the novel, Amyas Leigh is very much himself. Yet, as the godson of Grenville and a voyager with Drake, he is an amalgam of both; and in the account of events at La Guayra, he also bears analogies with Captain Amyas Preston. Also heroic and remaining his own idealistic self, Frank Leigh combines Raleigh and Philip Sidney, while Eustace Leigh is 'the very Ballard who was hanged and quartered . . . for his share in Babington's villainous conspiracy'. These and other parallels are managed so smoothly that fact and fiction blend with convincing felicity.

Parallels and similarities suggest contrasts and dissimilarities, and Kingsley also uses the principle of opposites in developing his plot. There are the basic oppositions between England and Spain, between Protestant and Catholic, like that between the stealthy and elusive Eustace Leigh and the fanatical Anabaptist, Salvation Yeo, who finds it 'against [his] conscience to be sworn'. There is also the more subtle opposition, quite irreconcilable, between those adventurers who acquisitively seek treasure for themselves, and those who, in the course of duty, take it as the lawful prize of Queen and country. A more improbable opposition is that set up between Amyas and Ayacanora, the reconciliation between whom, though carefully worked out, is only partially successful.

More fundamental is the opposition between Amyas and Eustace, of whom Kingsley comments that he is depicting 'two opposite sorts of men'. Eustace tries 'to be good . . . according to certain approved methods and rules', while Amyas simply does 'the right thing without thinking about it'. The former is trammelled by the Catholic system and the harsh demands of Jesuitical obedience; while the latter, rather like Coleridge's Asra, is naturally good by the grace of God. As the hero, Amyas is 'a son of God', whereas Eustace, the anti-hero and the villain preoccupied with 'the safety of his soul', never learns the meaning of 'divine self-sacrifice'. Between the two, Kingsley explains, a 'great gulf' is fixed, and like the Elizabethan polarization of 'Popery' and the Reformed faith, no reconciliation is possible.

Conversion, then, contributes to the plot of *Westward Ho!*, and the process is applied in Amyas's portrayal. Kingsley's usual golden-haired Hercules, Amyas resembles Tom Thurnall in *Two Years Ago*, but unlike that hearty gentleman, who is 'godless' (unconverted) throughout the greater part of the novel, Amyas is regenerate 'because the Spirit of God is with him'. Under the tutelage of Puritanical men like Grenville[34] and Drake, Amyas goes round the world, returns, and serves in Ireland with unquestioning trust in God. Drake had trained him to be stout in discipline and dogged of purpose, with feeling for his men. 'A symbol of young England', he finds his treasure, like Drake's[35] is 'not gold, but character', which enables him to turn every force to account, and to elicit the best from those who come within the sphere of his influence. His frankness is as treasured as his fearlessness and daring.

But Amyas is not perfect. He falls a prey to a particularly invidious kind of selfishness and his character deteriorates as a consequence. In terms of the plot the diastolic aspect of conversion enables Kingsley to dramatize his hero's fall from grace and public duty. Amyas's defection from godliness begins with his knowledge of Rose Salterne's elopement with Don Guzman for, fearing that her honour has been 'stained and ruined', Amyas curses the Spaniard and determines to have 'his heart's blood'. When chivalry demands the fulfilment of their oath, Frank is prompted by love and idealism whereas Amyas is moved by a desire for revenge. When Frank is lost at La Guayra this feeling is intensified and 'a terrible calm' settles upon him as he directs the attack on the Spanish ship with unwonted vengeance, and utter disregard for his men. His conscience smites him later, however, when he takes the loss of his brother as 'God's verdict' because he had set 'his own private affection, even his own private revenge, before the safety of his ship's company, and the good of his country' (Ch. xx, 373).

Nevertheless, hatred conquers. When the captured *City of the True Cross* yields up her awful secret regarding the deaths of Frank and Rose, and the Bishop of Carthagena has been hanged for his complicity in the affair, Amyas vows before God and his ship's company to hunt down Spaniards 'as long as [he has] eyes to see' and, determined to avenge his brother's death, he turns to 'dark purposes of revenge'. His whole soul gradually fills with a sullen hatred of Don Guzman, and he enters more and more into 'the darkness in which every man walks who hates his brother'. When the sea-fight with the Armada is under way and the *Rose* had been replaced by the *Vengeance*, Amyas can think neither of

'England's present need' nor of 'his own safety', but only of 'his brother's blood', increasingly required for the satisfaction of his revenge. He gets leave to pursue the *St. Catharine* and when, owing to his ruthless chase, she founders on the Shutter off Lundy and sinks with all on board, Amyas feels that God has deprived him of his personal right to destroy his enemy, and in a frenzy of anger, he hurls his sword 'far into the sea'.

Familiar with Kingsley's handling of diastolic patterns in other novels, we need not belabour this one. Amyas's vow is an example of Kingsley's careful plotting. Not until Amyas is struck blind by a flash of lightning at the same moment that the *St. Catharine* founders and sinks does the hero give up his pursuit. Contributing to Kingsley's schematic parallels, the same flash that strikes Amyas kills the faithful Yeo, whose attitude to Spain has everywhere run parallel to his Captain's. Thematically, too, the episode is a powerful dramatization of the refusal to walk *secundum Deum*. If Oxenham and Hawkins had perished in their attempt to put private gain before Queen and country, so now Amyas is punished for his blasphemy.

For a happy ending, however, Kingsley fortunately makes his hero repent of his wilfulness and pride:

'You do not repent of fighting the Spaniards'.
'Not I: but of hating even the worst of them. Listen to me, ... If that man [Don Guzman] wronged me, I wronged him likewise. I have been a fiend when I thought myself the grandest of men, yea a very avenging angel out of heaven. But God has shown me my sin, and we have made up our quarrel for ever'.[36]

Of an age that polarized Protestant and Catholic dispensations, and in a country that opted for the former, Kingsley reminds his own generation that the Spirit is at work everywhere. Love to God and neighbour is fundamental and contains all creeds. While the Catholic 'system' of the Elizabethan age with its implacable Holy Office of Inquisition had to go, much that was basic to the fabric of society had equally to be preserved. Little wonder that Queen Elizabeth vacillated in steering the ship of state. For those who would label *Westward Ho!* an anti-Catholic novel it must be urged that in his delineation of the Spanish nobleman Kingsley draws a

character consistently Christian and, as Amyas resumes his re-
generate life at the close of the novel, though blind, he sees that God
alone is Judge, that only in resignation to Him and in concord with
his enemy can he honour his oath:

'And I saw him sitting in his cabin, like a valiant gentleman of Spain;
and his officers were sitting round him, with their swords upon the table
at the wine. And the prawns and the crayfish and the rockling, they swam
in and out above their heads: but Don Guzman he never heeded, but
sat still, and drank his wine. Then he took a locket from his bosom; and
I heard him speak, Will, and he said: 'Here's the picture of my fair and
true lady; drink to her, Senors all.' Then he spoke to me, Will, and
called me, right up through the oar-weed and the sea: 'We have had a
fair quarrel, Senor; it is time to be friends once more. My wife and your
brother have forgiven me; so your honour takes no stain.' And I answered,
'We are friends, Don Guzman; God has judged our quarrel, and not we.'
Then he held out his hand to me, Cary; and I stooped to take it, and
awoke'.[37]

This vision is effective as neither of the dream sequences in *Yeast*
or *Alton Locke* has been, and the reference to their continuing
friendship introduces a fresh interpretation of Christian social
ethics.

Kingsley's portrayal of Queen Elizabeth is closer to the Gloriana
of *The Faerie Queene* than to the scheming tyrant of history.
The missions inspiring Kingsley's gentlemen adventurers are
analogous to those quests of the knights in Gloriana's court, and
the theme of glory as the result of a virtuous performance of duty
is the theme of the novel as it is of the poem.

A mirror of the time, *The Faerie Queene* offered a perfect model
for Kingsley's purposes: 'The temper of the Leighs and their
mother', he declared, 'is the same which inspires every canto of
that noblest of poems' (Ch. XVI, 310). He wrote a novel as heroic as
Spenser's poem because, like Carlyle, he believed the gentleman-
hero to play a significant part in history.[38] He also believed the
practice of the virtues to be fundamental to heroism. As the 'general
end' of *The Faerie Queene* was the fashioning of a noble person in
'vertuous and gentle discipline', so in *Westward Ho!* Kingsley
upholds those virtues which go to the making of a chivalric and

noble gentleman, and he commends them to the nineteenth-century world of action. 'Let us open our eyes', he writes,

and see in these old Elizabethan gallants our own ancestors, showing forth . . . all the virtues which still go to the making of a true Englishman. Let us not only see in their commercial and military daring, in their political astuteness, in their deep reverence for law, and in their solemn sense of the great calling of the English nation, the examples of our own: but let us confess that their chivalry is only another garb of that beautiful tenderness and mercy which is now, as it was then, the twin sister of English valour (Ch. VIII, 159).

Virtue is necessary for chivalry and chivalry, in turn, demands the exercise of mercy in human relationships.

Virtue is vital for heroism and, conversely, the hero is 'a man elevated above the human condition by a burning love of virtue'.[39] 'It is virtue, yea virtue . . . that maketh a gentleman', Lyly declares in *Euphues*, to which Kingsley referred for an epigraph to head his chapter on the founding of the brotherhood. Sidney's *Arcadia* is equally concerned with virtue and justice, teaching that patience and magnanimity, 'like man and woman, are opposite and yet complementary' and that co-operation between them leads to perfection.[40]

In the fourth book of *The Faerie Queene*, Kingsley found friendship put forward as a relationship presupposing virtue and chivalry, and therefore as being akin to the ideas that he and Maurice had advanced as Christian socialism. Because they were theologians, their ideas emerged in a religious context, but in his novels where Kingsley relates them to the life of his characters they are given a secular cast within a religious framework; and in *Westward Ho!* Kingsley supports them, not only with authors whose writings were contemporaneous with the period of his novel, but also with the sources upon which they themselves had drawn.[41]

In the *Nicomachean Ethics* Aristotle defined friendship as the attractive principle in human nature, and made it a social phenomenon;[42] and Spenser, who knew Aristotle's work, appears to have profited also from Francesco Piccolomini, who compared *amicitia* with Aristotle's *philia*, explaining that it gave affability and humanity to Aristotle's active principle of friendship. Piccolomini defined friendship as the 'mutual, open, and confirmed love of upright men, rising from a recognition of uprightness and leading to a conjunction of honest life' and, like Aristotle, he insists that the love in friendship is prompted by virtue, and manifests itself in actions proceeding from it 'as though rays from the sun'.

Spenser adapted these ideas to his treatment of friendship in *The Faerie Queene* where he specifies three kinds of love and prefers the 'zeale of friends combynd in vertues meet' before either of the others. 'Faithful friendship', because it arises directly from the practice of virtue, 'the gentle hart should most assured bind'[43] and Kingsley's Christian socialism in *Westward Ho!* becomes a dramatization of it. Relying on free will in the active exercise of virtue, friendship evokes trust, loyalty, and honour, giving rise to the chivalry and mercy which, for Kingsley, are enshrined in valour.

The importance of the Brotherhood of the Rose as a structural device has already been shown. In terms of Kingsley's teaching, it is the key-note of his theme as well. The six young men whom the Leigh brothers invite to the Ship Tavern are, together with themselves, all contenders for the Rose. If there must be rivalry among them, however, it is to be 'a rivalry of nobleness, an emulation in virtue', and the pledge of brotherhood is an assurance of their concerted effort and continuous amity. 'The health of the Rose of Torridge', Frank cries, lifting his glass aloft, 'and a double health to that worthy gentleman, . . . whom she is fated to honour with her love!' After Kingsley in the guise of Frank has preached his sermon on Christian brotherhood, the company rises to 'join hands all round, and swear eternal friendship, as brothers of the sacred order of the Rose'. In their allegiance to her each man rises beyond personal and competitive interest to deeds which will bring honour, not only to her, but to them as well. 'Let each try to outstrip the other in loyalty to his queen, in valour against her foes, in deeds of courtesy and mercy to the afflicted and oppressed', declares Kingsley through the mouthpiece of his Elizabethan courtier, 'and thus our love will indeed prove its own divine origin' (Ch. VIII, 164). Transferred to Gloriana and her Court, the concept of unanimity in action for the building of the kingdom (alike of

England and of Christ) is powerfully impressed, and the significance
for the Crimean effort was tremendous. 'Glory follows virtue like
a shadow'.

As contrast contributed to structure, so it strengthens theme.
Popularizing Spenser as he had popularized Maurice, Kingsley
reviewed the difference between true chivalry and false, between
heroic knighthood and blundering folly; the difference, in a word,
between Spenser's Red Cross knight and Cervantes' Don Quixote
who, instead of seeing the world as 'a battlefield for heroes in God's
cause', found it no more than a place of 'frivolity, heartlessness,
and godlessness'.[44] Frank Leigh is no scoffer, but his idealism is so
misplaced and other-worldly that the brothers' attack on the
Governor's residence at La Guayra cannot succeed. At the crucial
moment when Frank is ready to sacrifice his life to save Rose from
the Inquisition, Amyas, 'for the first and last time in his life' is
'irresolute'. Frank is captured, for the whole venture is one of
'mistaken chivalry'. However noble Frank's love for Rose she, after
all, has chosen another; and Amyas, on his side, had diverted public
duty to private ends. Indeed, their action is not unlike that of the
hapless six hundred who, though riding 'boldly' and 'well', rode
'Into the jaws of Death/Into the mouth of Hell' – heroically,
perhaps, but pointlessly. Not even Tennyson can hide the tragedy
behind their brave but false show of honour.

Nor are parallel adaptations lacking. As Britomart promises not
to see Artegal '. . . till the horned moon three courses [does]
expire',[45] so in the novel the brotherhood vow neither to see the
Rose nor hear tidings of her 'till three full years are past'. The
parallel may be extended to fiction and history. When the brotherhood scatter to the ends of the earth the Rose is left to the un-
contested courtship of Don Guzman and, equally, with Queen
Elizabeth's knights abroad on every sea, all Europe anticipates
marriage between the Queen and Henry of Anjou, or another of the
Catholic contenders for the royal hand; in which case, she and her
England would have 'burned' at the stake as do Rose and Frank.

In Spenser's poem Artegal plays a part similar to that of Amyas
in the novel, and both bear analogies with Essex and other Elizabethan knights who served in Ireland. Artegal 'must save the lady

Eirena (Ireland) from the clutches of Grantorto (Spain)' and, as one of the royal line of Celts, she 'lives in two centuries, the sixth and the sixteenth, in one as an actual historical personage, in the other as a reincarnation [in Spenser's poem] after a lapse of a thousand years'.[46] The parallel between the historical figure and the fictional reincarnation applies not only to Kingsley's imposition of the sixteenth century upon the nineteenth, but to the historical leap in his reading of history from the fifth to the sixteenth. And just as Artegal redeems Ireland from Spain for 'the timeless land' of Faerie, so does Amyas in Kingsley's novel: 'Remember', says Raleigh, addressing Spenser on the subject of Amyas, 'you may write about Fairyland, but he has seen it'. 'And so have others', replies Spenser: 'wherever is love and loyalty, great purposes, and lofty souls, even though in a hovel or a mine, there is Fairyland'.[47]

The Amyas-Rose-Frank triangle illustrates the principle of association on which the Christian socialists were so intent in 1848. In planning the brotherhood with Frank, Amyas reveals goodwill and amity, and thus a growth in the chivalric ideal. He passes the first test of love, that of kinship. He passes the second also in sublimating his love for Rose by going off to Ireland and relinquishing her to Frank. The brotherhood is duly founded, thereby demonstrating the growth of social concord from the family nucleus. But Amyas fails the third test when he neglects to honour his pledge to the gentleman whom Rose is 'fated to honour with her love'.

Kingsley wrote *Westward Ho!* to commemorate 'the glorious fight of 1588' and to honour the 'forgotten worthies' whose voyages and battles, faith and heroism had saved England for freedom to mould the next stage of history and, with this in mind, he dedicated *Westward Ho!* to two worthy contemporaries, the Rajah Sir James Brooke, and George Augustus Selwyn, first Bishop of New Zealand.[48] These men exhibited, he said, 'that type of English virtue, at once manful and godly, practical and enthusiastic, prudent and self-sacrificing', surpassing that which he had depicted in his novel and even that exhibited by the worthies whom Queen Elizabeth had gathered round her 'in the ever glorious wars of her great reign'.

As Rajah of Sarawak, Sir James Brooke (1803-68) suppressed piracy and headhunting in the Malayan Archipelago but, in spite of his success, his efforts brought charges of inhumanity and illegal conduct, in the House of Commons. Although honoured by the City of London, Oxford University, and Queen Victoria when he returned to England in 1847, and although appointed British Commissioner in Borneo, the Commission of Inquiry impaired his authority among the natives with the result that Chinese immigrants attacked Government House and he narrowly escaped being murdered. As primate of New Zealand and bishop of Lichfield, Selwyn (1809–78), on the other hand, carried out a thorough visitation of the whole of New Zealand and, in 1854 when Kingsley was writing *Westward Ho!*, returned to England with plans for the self-government of his diocese, and he thus established the legal constitution of the church in New Zealand. Both men were carrying on the tradition of Elizabethan heroes, and if Kingsley's style bubbles with optimism bordering on pomposity, it is to be remembered that the spacious days of Queen Elizabeth were assuredly more spacious for Victorians, who accepted their Empire with an unwavering sense of duty and commitment.

Westward Ho! hymns brotherly concord, love and romance; and the book promulgates faith in the 'brave new world'. But as in *The Faerie Queene*, so in Kingsley's novel a gentle melancholy warns readers to watchfulness and the need to discriminate between good and evil, right and wrong and Kingsley, like Spenser, preaches the age-old themes because conscience and common sense know them to be true. A paean in praise of patriotism, *Westward Ho!* is also a plea for courage and godliness.

CHAPTER 7

Two Years Ago

'My fairest child', protested Charles Kingsley when Miss Charlotte Grenfell asked him to write in her album, 'I have no song to give you'. He was thinking of themes for *Two Years Ago* – of the cholera and the Crimean war – and could not 'pipe to skies so dull and grey'. But no sooner had he penned this rueful negation than the resolute preacher countered the poet with 'one lesson . . . for every day':

> Be good, sweet maid, and let who will be clever,
> Do noble things, not dream them, all day long,
> So making life, death, and that vast forever,
> One grand, sweet song.[1]

Hastily dashed off in his niece's souvenir book, this wistful farewell song proclaims the theme of all Kingsley's writings, and in none more forthrightly than in *Two Years Ago*. Disarmingly simple, yet transcending the usual triviality of album verses, these lines are an epigraph for the whole novel.

Both are buttressed by Christian social theory. *Yeast* and *Alton Locke* urged co-operation among the working classes, but *Two Years Ago* imposes it upon all. Like death stalking through the land, the cholera has come 'to flesh his teeth in every kind of prey' and sanitation has become a momentous issue. Cleanliness alone can keep the dreaded disease at bay and the co-operation needed to accomplish this embraces the nation at large. Cleanliness means healthier, cleaner minds,[2] and this depends upon lively consciences inspiring action on behalf of national decency and order.

For Coleridge, Maurice, and Kingsley the conscience is the man himself, who, informed by the 'divine word',[3] has a built-in knowledge of the good and the right. The conscience, indeed, is a 'testifying state' arising from the 'coincidence of the human will with reason and religion' so that the will becomes the reconciling agent between right thinking and Christian practice. In *The*

Kingdom of Christ Maurice defined the will as a faculty which could only exist in 'going out of itself', and thus it translates man's reasonable knowledge of God into action manifesting Him. In obedience to the 'divine word', the will is none other than 'the intense sense of a vocation to help and instruct others'.

Because the church aids in *well-doing* while the state enforces *well-being*, Maurice saw the whole fabric of society as assisting each man to be and to do, and with his unique gift for popularizing his mentor, Kingsley aptly inculcates his teaching here.[4] In terms of individual action, 'good' results when, instead of dreaming about it, the will transforms the dream of 'doing' into the reality of noble things 'done', so that being and doing commingle in 'doing right', and in *Two Years Ago* Kingsley dramatizes human relationships that contribute to righteousness. 'What else is life . . . but deeds?', Major Campbell asks Valencia St. Just as he rouses her to action, and goes on to remind her that only to the extent of one's helpfulness to others does one become God-like. It is nobler to live for one's countrymen than to die for one's country.

Kingsley began the third volume of *Westward Ho!* (Ch. XXI) with Amyas Leigh's ship in a tropical mangrove swamp. Reeking with pestilence and fever, it evokes comments from the crew, all of which suggested a further book on the subject of sanitation, namely *Two Years Ago*:

The doctor talked mere science, or nonscience, about humours, complexions, and animal spirits. Jack Brimblecombe [the chaplain] mere pulpit, about its being the visitation of God. Cary, mere despair, though he jested over it with a smile, Yeo [the evangelical gunner], mere stoic fatalism, though he quoted Scripture to back the same. Drew, the master, had nothing to say. His 'business was to sail the ship, and not to cure calentures'.[5]

These attitudes are all expressed and amplified in *Two Years Ago*.

The novel is disappointing. It suggests the pious parson in his pulpit and savours too much of a long and tedious Victorian sermon. Lacking the fire of *Yeast* and *Alton Locke*, it also fails to impart the vision and scope of *Hypatia* and *Westward Ho!* and, although Kingsley was both prolific and popular by 1857, he regarded the novel as altogether 'a farce and a sham', which a parson ought not to condone,[6] and something of this feeling pervades the book.

The first edition of the novel appeared in the three volumes familiar to Victorians. The first included the opening ten chapters of the one-volume edition in the *Works* (VIII), the second carried the story forward to the end of Chapter XVIII, and the third, the remaining ten. The novel also contains a prologue, consisting of introductory matter and the first chapter, which sets the background of the tale in Whitbury, Berkshire, and which introduces the principal characters, Tom Thurnall and John Briggs, sixteen years before the story proper begins. Aged eighteen, both youths are on the threshold of their respective careers, and the story begins as Tom Thurnall the hero, and John Briggs the anti-hero, are about to leave Whitbury. The action takes place in the West Country but the closing chapters converge on Whitbury again as the last scene fades into the background.

The historical situation places the characters in perspective. The Crimean war had broken out on 27 March, 1854,[7] and, with Gladstone feeling that it would 'swallow up everything good and useful', Britain had despatched an expeditionary force of 30,000 men. Meanwhile, 'the most terrible outbreak' of cholera which had ever occurred in the kingdom fell upon London and Oxford;[8] and no sooner had the epidemic been brought under control at home than it reached alarming proportions in the theatre of war.[9]

In London, cholera struck Golden Square with 'fearful, inexplicable, and fatal violence'. J. M. Ludlow and Thomas Hughes, assisting Dr. D. Fraser in a house-to-house visitation, examined drains and sanitary arrangements in an attempt to discover both the causes of the disease and its mode of dissemination.[10] They published the results of their work in a pamphlet supplementing both Dr. Southwood Smith's *Results of Sanitary Improvements* (1853) and John Snow's *On the Mode of Communication of Cholera* (1855). Meanwhile, having settled his family in Bideford for the winter of 1854, Kingsley visited houses in a district where forty-six deaths had occurred,[11] and to his sojourn there may be attributed the setting of *Two Years Ago*.

Oxford seems to have been peculiarly vulnerable with an attack in 1832, a sharper one in 1849, and a third in the autumn of 1854.[12] Sir Henry Acland was the Regius Professor of medicine in the university, and was assisted by Professor Max Muller, who suddenly became his patient; but as Kingsley's close friend, Acland supplied him with first-hand information and, as the husband of his niece, Max Muller kept him in touch as well. During the 1849 epidemic Acland had been hampered by 'an unfortunate disagreement between the Guardians and the Board of Health', so that it had become imperative to establish authority for methods of procedure in the event of future epidemics. With a free hand in 1854, Acland published his small but important *Memoir on the Cholera at Oxford in the Year 1854* and one of Kingsley's purposes in *Two Years Ago* was the popular dissemination of Acland's findings. The subject was of interest to him as a Christian socialist and, Acland, like Kingsley, believed morality to be inseparable from social welfare.[13] Local Guardians, like those at Oxford, were too often parsimonious and apathetic, hiding behind the cloak of Kingsley's *bête noire*, *laissez-faire*,[14] and he turned this to account in his novel.

Whitbury has been likened to Eversley, and while this may be so, it is also the Whitford of the Lavington's who in *Yeast* were the 'great folks of the priory'. Lord Minchampstead's new schools and model cottages are now a practical proof of the growing improvements in the country, and Mark Armsworth fills Squire Lavington's place in the community. His oldest and closest friend is Edward Thurnall, the local doctor 'beloved and trusted by rich and poor alike', and the father of Tom. These two characters are pillars of strength for Tom and John, who never forget Whitbury in their vicissitudes.

Armsworth is the local banker and railway-director, the '*de facto* king of Whitbury town' and in passing, it is scarcely to be doubted that this description of him is a compliment to Kingsley's brother-in-law, George Carr Glyn, banker, and a patron of George Stephenson the inventor of the Rocket. Glyn was later Chairman of the North-western railway and in 1869 became first Baron Wolverton, taking his title from the important town on the railway. He had married Mrs. Kingsley's elder sister, Marianne, in 1823.

The action takes place, not in Whitbury, but in Aberalva, and all other places find their importance in relation to it: Beddgelert and Snowdon in Wales, Ehrenbreitstein in Germany; Sebastopol, Scutari, and Alma in the Crimea; and Whitbury itself. Aberalva is a fishing village and Kingsley describes the harbour at low tide when 'a dozen trawlers are lopping over on their sides'. Readers climb the single street step by step as it rises from the harbour to Penalva Court at the top of the cliff. To this town Tom is brought as the sole survivor in a shipwreck off the coast, and in the rescue operation, he loses his belt containing the Australian money intended for his blind and ageing father in Whitbury. Tom temporarily settles as old Dr. Heale's assistant, and thus Kingsley fixes the setting for his tale.

Meanwhile, Tom meets the townsfolk – Grace Harvey, the beautiful and saintly schoolmistress with whom he falls in love; Frank Headley, the Puseyite curate, who is bent on maintaining 'church principles' in a largely Brianite Methodist community; and Elsley Vavasour, the self-centred poet who lives, thanks to his wife's connexion with the absentee landlord Viscount Scoutbush, at Penalva Court.

The town is 'fair without and foul within'. The gutter in the centre of the single street is the common sewer and owing to this and other unsavoury conditions disease and pestilence descend upon the little town during the dry summer of 1854. An 'awful unseen presence' with an 'appetite more fierce than ever', king cholera sweeps into Aberalva:

. . . up the main street he goes unabashed springing in at one door and at another, on either side of the street. . . . He fleshes his teeth on every kind of prey. The drunken cobbler dies, of course: but spotless cleanliness and sobriety does not save the mother of seven children, who had been soaking her brick floor with water from a poisoned well, defiling where she meant to clean. Youth does not save the buxom lass, who has been filling herself, as girls will do, with unripe fruit: nor innocence the two fair children who were sailing their feather-boats yesterday in the quay-pools, as they have sailed them for three years past, and found no hurt: piety does not save the bed-ridden old dame . . . in the lean-to garret, who moans, 'It is the Lord!' and dies (Ch. XVII, 300).

Tom calls for help as innocence and piety, youth and age are all cut down. Headley and Major Campbell, Grace Harvey and old Captain Willis, and last, but not least, Tom himself, form 'a right-gallant and well-disciplined band', and start a visitation from house to house. Tom and Grace toil day and night to heal the sick and comfort the dying throughout a weary siege that ends in Aberalva only to be renewed in the Crimea a thousand miles away. These 'two good people', forced by the horrors of cholera to believe that God is love, 'Do noble things, not dream them, all day long, . . .'

Two Years Ago is a fiction, and Aberalva a figment of the imagination. Examining the novel for its social implications, one speculates on the actual town that Kingsley had in mind. Aberalva is thought to be Clovelly, and this Devonshire fishing village is almost certainly the place described. Kingsley naturally drew on his knowledge of the parish where he had spent the happiest years of his boyhood but, aiming at universality, he kept to the West Country generally. When the cholera arrives (Chapter XVIII), Tavistock is specifically mentioned as the centre of the 'plague-struck land'. There is no record of an epidemic there, however, and while Clovelly escaped in 1854, Bideford suffered a severe attack in which, as we know, Kingsley had assisted the local authorities.

His *genre* left him free to select both times and places, and to organize his material in a manner most suited to his purpose. Though Devon is undoubtedly depicted, many of the descriptions in *Two Years Ago* suggest Cornwall, and many of the names assigned to the characters have a Cornish flavour. Aberalva may conceivably be Mevagissey.[15] A Cornish fishing village situated 'in a valley without proper drainage', it was the scene of a severe epidemic in 1849. The local doctor, behaving like Tom Thurnall, promptly obtained tents and 'set up a camp half a mile away at Port Mellon, where there was a supply of fresh water' and as a result, only those who elected to stay in the town contracted the cholera, and of these nearly 140 died.

Childhood events in Helston may also colour the novel. While Kingsley was a schoolboy under the Rev. Derwent Coleridge he suffered 'a violent attack of English cholera' and, although the highly sensitive boy bore up bravely, his illness 'occasioned the more alarm' because the 'Asiatic form' of the disease had come and his illness was inevitably associated with it. At Helston, too, his brother Herbert, afflicted with 'a severe attack of rheumatism', suddenly suffered a heart attack and died, giving Charles a great shock and causing him inexpressible grief.[16] As the Bristol riots were turned to account in *Alton Locke*, so these traumatic incidents in Helston tinge *Two Years Ago*.

As for his characters, Kingsley merely put his own experience into their mouths,[17] but before turning to them it may be well to recall the experiences themselves. In the first days of Christian social enthusiasm Kingsley had seen that filth and poverty went hand in hand and when he and his friends had made their memorable visit to Jacob's Island they were convinced that sanitation was imperative. Kingsley was greatly disturbed by the foulness he had seen, and roused his Christian socialist friends and men of influence to immediate action.

At his request Ludlow had written to the Chairman of the Bermondsey Improvement Commission, while he himself had urged his brother-in-law, Lord Sidney Godolphin Osborne, to send a letter to *The Times*; the Hon. and Rev. Rector of Durweston had also published *Immortal Sewerage* (1853), in which he had bewailed the '*moral miasmas*' which were caused by physical ones.[18] Kingsley had also obtained an interview with Wilberforce, the Bishop of Oxford who, in turn, had urged him to get in touch with Lord Carlisle and Lord John Russell. He had also been one of a deputation to Lord Palmerston on sanitation, and he had addressed the House on the subject.

Some of the Christian socialists had wished to make their first priority a Health League. Although they abandoned the plan, they collected twenty pounds to start a water-cart in the district, and some of the men had volunteered to serve out the water. Eventually they installed 'stout oak casks with brass cocks to provide a reserve supply',[19] and Bermondsey was thus an *experimentum crucis*.

Kingsley's immediate and most satisfactory response, however, had been a series of sermons on the cholera, the first of which was preached at Eversley on 27 September, 1849. He had dwelt on the earlier epidemic of 1832, and had argued that morality demanded action for sanitation. 'Being good' meant 'doing good' which, in this instance, meant a general scouring of houses and the willing assumption of responsibility for seeing it done. As Eversley tidied itself up the sermons were 'peppered for London palates and prepared for the press' in the hope of stimulating similar activity everywhere.

The real sins were indifference and procrastination. As Kingsley had declared, fifteen years had passed since the Sanitary Commissioners had proved that cholera and fever always appeared together, and that both inevitably clung to places where there were foul air and poor drainage. This was a common-sense law of nature, he had explained, and had gone on to tell his parishioners that they had all wilfully ignored it to their own harm. They had suffered a second visitation (1849) because they had been covetous, tyrannical, and careless, and because they had blindly refused to heed the lesson provided by the earlier visitation. Now in 1854 it was again time for action, time to clean and drain the stifling hovels which, though 'unfit for hogs', still housed many of the poor. Now, for the third time, the danger was upon them. Would they rise to their duty?

Behind the indifference lay superstition. In a lecture on the subject delivered at the Royal Institution (1867) Kingsley identified superstition or false belief with fear, as he had always done. Spiritual fear, the fear of 'doing wrong' was both moral and praiseworthy. But superstitious fear was carnal and operated among the unthinking, who identified the thing symbolized with the symbol itself. For the majority of them, the pestilence was not an evil to be met and overcome by sanitation. It was a Visitation against which it was blasphemy to contend. Seized with blind fear, these people thought only of themselves, and were thus consumed by their own selfishness, Kingsley declared.

As the third visitation struck the kingdom, he republished his sermons as a tract, *Who Causes the Pestilence?* introducing them with a preface in which he deplored inactivity, apathy, and fear. The passivity only fostered the scourge, he said, and he approved of Lord Palmerston's refusal to allow a national fast day. Everybody knew how to extirpate the evil, he declared, and God now demanded action instead of prayers.[20] As 1854 was drawing to a close and the ravages before Sebastopol were haunting him day and night he dashed off his latter-day pamphlet, *Brave Words to Brave Soldiers*, and as we have seen, sent thousands of copies to the Crimea.[21] Then, finishing off *Westward Ho!* to remind the soldiers of their glorious heritage and inspire them with confidence and patriotism in the face of the foe, Kingsley turned to his drama on sanitation.

Two Years Ago humanizes all the ideas found in the sermons. Each character is given a set of feelings and attitudes with which to respond to the epidemic and Kingsley's contemporaries saw themselves mirrored as each plays his part in the novel. In 'The Doctor at Bay' (Ch. XIV) Tom, convinced that the cholera is coming, tries 'his best to persuade people to get ready for their ugly visitor; but in vain'. He approaches Tardrew (Viscount Scoutbush's steward), old Dr. Heale, Headley the curate, Elsley the dreaming poet, and Valencia St. Just who, as Lucia Vavasour's sister, is asked to write to the Viscount.

None can help. Tardrew thinks Tom a veritable busy-body, either 'very silly' or 'very impertinent'; old Dr. Heale, the Bible in hand and echoing the Brianite preacher whom Tom has already offended, sees the visitation as 'a judgment of God'; in response to Valencia's letter, Scoutbush replies a full fortnight later that his tenants have 'copyholds and long leases' over which he has no control, and he can do nothing. As for the tenants, the most influential of them, the fish salesman Treludda who combines money-lending with business, has fish in his back-yard 'in every stage of putrefaction', which he prefers to keep rotting there rather than lower the market-price. Tom very nearly has fisticuffs with him but desists, knowing that a public brawl will not help the cause.

At last, Tom defies the local Guardians and writes to the Board of Health informing them civilly that the Nuisance Removal Act is simply 'waste paper' in Aberalva. But even they dare not interfere until cholera has actually broken out. It is at this point that Kingsley, falling to the level of invective used in *Yeast* and *Alton Locke*, acidly comments on *laissez-faire*:

And so was Aberalva left 'a virgin city' undefiled by Government inter-
ference, to the blessings of the 'local government', which signifies, in

plain English, the leaving the few to destroy themselves and the many, by the unchecked exercise of the virtues of pride and ignorance, stupidity and stinginess (Ch. xIV, 224).

Then, invective mingles with prophecy as his uneven style waxes Biblical:

But the wind came not, nor the rain; and the cholera crept nearer and nearer: while the hearts of all in Aberalva were hardened, and out of very spite against the agitators, they did less than they would have done otherwise (Ch. xv, 283).

A 'virgin city' Aberalva remains until 'sportively' the cholera comes. Tom Beer, 'one of the finest fellows in the town' is struck down. In two hours he is dead (Ch. xvi). The next day there are three more cases: the day after, thirteen (Ch. xvii); and to the pestilence is added the fear of eternal punishment – the superstitious emotion that hastens on the epidemic.

Only two people are willing to help Tom – Frank Headley and Grace Harvey. But because of his 'Church principles', which are abhorrent to the majority of the townsfolk, Frank can do nothing. Frank *is*, and therefore ought, in Christian terms, to *do* good. Replying to Tom's order to 'preach', Headley meekly replies that the church is opposed to purely secular subjects in the pulpit; and at this point, in one of the weakest parts of the book, the novel sinks to tract level as the yet unchristian doctor Tom preaches the Christian High-church curate a Christian Socialist sermon.

Flung upon the page in Kingsley's usual precipitate haste, it is worthy of ample quotation.

'. . . don't you put up the Ten Commandments in your Church?'
'Yes'.
'And don't [sic] one of them run: "Thou shalt not kill"?'
'Well?'
'And is not murder a moral offence – what you call a sin?'
'*Sans doute*'.
'If you saw your parishioners in the habit of cutting each other's throats, or their own, shouldn't you think that a matter spiritual enough to be a fit subject for a little of the drum ecclesiastic?'
'Well?'
'Well? Ill! There are your parishioners about to commit wholesale murder and suicide, and is that a secular question? If they don't know

the fact, is not that all the more reason for your telling them of it? . . .
Why on earth do you hold your tongue about the sins of which they are
not aware? You tell us every Sunday that we do Heaven only knows how
many more wrong things than we dream of. Tell it us again now. Don't
strain at gnats like the want of faith and resignation, and swallow such a
camel as twenty or thirty deaths . . . if it's not your concern, what on
earth you are here for is more than I can tell'. 'You are right – you are
right; but how to put it on religious grounds –' Tom whistled again.
'If your doctrines cannot be made to fit such plain matters as twenty
deaths, *tant pis pour eux*. If they have nothing to say on such scientific
facts, why the facts must take care of themselves, and the doctrines may,
for aught I care, go and – But I won't be really rude. Only think over
the matter: if you are God's minister, you ought to have something
to say about God's view of a fact which certainly involves the lives of
his creatures, not by twos and threes, but by tens of thousands' (Ch.
XIV, 217).

Frank went home and thought it through, Kingsley adds and,
as if young Tom had been a veritable Socrates, Headley went to
Thurnall again, and asked his

opinion of what he had said, and whether he said ill or well. What
Thurnall answered was – 'Whether that's sound Church doctrine is your
business; but if it be, I'll say, with the man there in the Acts – what was
his name? – "Almost thou persuadest me to be a Christian"' (Ch.
XIV, 217).

The man 'in the Acts' is of course St. Paul, and we are again reminded of *Yeast*.

In Chapter XVIII Kingsley again puts the cholera sermons into
Tom's mouth as the hero fulminates against the Brianite preacher,
whose enthusiasm contributes unnecessarily to the spread of the
epidemic:

'Why should I not curse and swear in the street', [gasps Tom excitedly],
'while every fellow who calls himself a preacher is allowed to do it in
the pulpit with impunity! Fine him five shillings for every curse, as you
might if people had courage and common sense. . . . To have all my
work undone by a brutal ignorant fanatic! – It is too much! Here,
if you will believe it, are those preaching fellows getting up a revival,
or some such invention, just to make money out of the cholera! They have
got down a great gun from the county town. Twice a day they are preaching at them, telling them that it is all God's wrath against their sins; that

it is impious to interfere, and that I am fighting against God, and the end of the world is coming, . . .'

'Is it possible? How did you find this out?'

'Mrs. Heale had been in, listening to their howling, just before she was taken. Heale went in when I turned him out of doors; came home raving mad, and is all but blue now. Three cases of women have I had this morning, all frightened into cholera, by their own confession, by last night's tomfoolery. – Came home howling, fainted, and were taken before morning. One is dead, the other two will die' (Ch. XVII, 305).

Unfair as this outburst must have seemed to contemporary Brianites and other sect groups, it was not mere prejudice. The Guardians of Oxford had been too parsimonious to allow Dr. Acland's patients the necessary food he had prescribed for them, and they were equally prejudiced against the removal of the sick to regular hospitals. Although arrangements in Aberalva – whether Clovelly, Bideford, Tavistock, or Mevagissey – differed widely from those in Oxford, the same appalling attitudes prevailed. West-country people had long since been under the evangelical spell of the Wesleys and the enthusiasm denounced by Tom is probably not greatly over-drawn despite allegations of prejudice on the part of contemporary nonconformist reviewers.[22]

Kingsley's source for his treatment of religious enthusiasm as contributable to the onslaught of the epidemic may have derived from his knowledge of events in Wales in 1849. Merthyr Tydfil and Denbigh has escaped very lightly in the first epidemic, but its terrifying recurrence there 'sparked off a remarkable religious revival'. Regarded as a "fearful preacher" ', the cholera drew vast throngs to local chapels at five o'clock in the morning.[23] Tom's outburst against excitement confirms the ill effects of superstition, for the clutching fear bred its own destruction. Although Tom has not yet been 'converted', he is closer to Christianity, the preacher is saying, than these people, captivated by superstition.

In *Two Years Ago* Kingsley applied the now familiar theme of conversion, less to the structural sequence as in *Yeast* and *Alton Locke*, than as a process of growth in the hero. Changes in character result from experience rather than preaching imposed by a saintly prophet or prophetess, as happens in the earlier works, and Tom's is a case in point. When the novel opens the jolly and uncomplicated hero is leaving for Paris to study medicine and four years later, having been half way round the world, he stops briefly in Whitbury on his way to Georgia to free a poor quadroon slave-girl for their friend, a Yankee surgeon whose dying wish in Circassia it was. Tom gets her away to Canada and gives her the money saved by her lover for her purchase, which she uses to study in London. La Cordifiamma – such is the Italianate name she adopts on the London stage – looks up to him as a hero, less because he has given her freedom, than because he is the only man she knows 'who, seeing the right, has gone and done it forthwith' (Ch. IX, 137). Tom is not only a man of action but a man of right action, and this is commendably heroic.

Like La Cordifiamma, Frank Headley also sees Tom in this light. Unsuccessful with his parishioners, Frank longs to acquire Tom's power of ' "becoming all things to all men" '. Tom has gained 'more real insight' into Frank's parishioners in one month than Frank has done in twelve and, because he is 'at heart a truly genuine man' with 'human strength', Tom's humanity finds theirs and, like St. Paul, he does 'what he proposes to do' (Ch. X, 171). Like St. Paul, he does God's work in spite of himself: 'Christ was of old the model, and Sir Galahad was the hero' (Ch. IX, 134).

The genuine hero is 'like the gods', and because he shares their nature he is expected 'to be a better man than common men', not so much in physical as in spiritual strength. His actions, which constitute conduct, are always tempered with that 'perfect respect for the feelings of others which spring out of perfect self-respect',[24] and Tom has most of these qualities.

But he is a braggart, high-handed and, at times, even truculent. Headley sees his double nature. On the one hand he is 'the most miraculously impudent of men', yet on the other, he is zealous in good works: 'You are always pretending to care for nothing but your own interest, and yet here you have gone out of your way to incur odium, knowing, you say, that your cause was all but hopeless', he remarks of Tom's work in Aberalva (Ch. XIV, 223).

Clearly, Tom is deficient spiritually. Though as moral as the 'average man', he is frankly 'ungodly' because he has no faith in a Being who can help him, not even a 'practical notion' of a heavenly

Father. His adventures have made him hard, calculating, and self-sufficient. He studies men shrewdly and weighs their weaknesses for his own ends; 'self-poised' and proud and, hardening himself into 'stoical security', he treads grievously on the feelings of others.

His ignoble tendency to use people soon degenerates into a desire for power over them, and in Dr. Heale's surgery he reveals 'suspicion and contempt' for many of the local citizens (Ch. v, 90). Among the first to fall foul of this dastardly quality is Elsley Vavasour, for Tom has recognized the evasive poet of Penalva Court as his old companion, John Briggs of Whitbury, who not only publishes, but has now married and lives under the assumed but poetic name of Vavasour. The scene of their confrontation in 'The Recognition' (Ch. x) reveals Tom in a very poor light, while the confinement chafes Elsley and contributes to his ruin.

In the equally important fourteenth chapter, Tom is 'at bay' on more counts than Christian socialism and sanitation. His proposal to Grace Harvey, the most intensely dramatic scene in the novel, is also bedevilled by his uncontrollable desire for dominion. He always suspected her of stealing his *rouleau*, which had actually been stolen by her mother rather than Grace, who had no knowledge of her mother's theft. As she struggles to free herself from his embrace, he ungallantly taunts her about it: 'Till that is at least restored, you are in my power, Grace! Remember that!' Though the words cut deeply, the saintly girl, whom he knows to be innocent, remains steadfast. Her love for him is exceeded only by her determination to find that belt.

In the end, her integrity and love came home to him in a Russian prison. In isolation his strength cannot save him; neither can his pride and cunning. Isolation forces him to face himself and, seeing himself, he sees Grace's devotion and selflessness the more startlingly by contrast, and his vision of her helps him to humility.

Not by accident is the heroine named 'grace'. More godly than Tom, she assists him to true heroism. The more he has attempted to restrain himself from 'prudential motives' of self sufficiency, the more 'sudden and violent' is his surrender.[25] As Saul became Paul, so the Carlylean becomes the Kingsleian hero as he approaches the ideal: again 'Christ was of old the model, and Sir Galahad was the hero'.

As a purely spiritual phenomenon, Tom's conversion is, like so many of Kingsley's conversions, something of a *tour de force*. It occurs too suddenly at the close of the novel to carry conviction. He failed to give any indication of its likelihood in the earlier love scene between Grace and Tom, and when the crucial moment in Tom's isolation comes, Grace is not present, so the reader must be content with the author's oblique report of it. None the less, he intended Tom's conversion to be the crowning glory as always, of an essentially heroic type dedicating himself completely to good works.

Tom's portrait, said to be modelled on Kingsley's brother George[26] who was a doctor, probably also owes something to the behaviour of the local doctor at Mevagissey. An equally strong influence on the drawing may have been the arduous work of a final-year medical student on holiday in Denbigh. Exhausted, Evan Pierce arrived from Scotland where he had been fighting the cholera, only to find himself caught up in the Denbigh epidemic. He coped so efficiently that he became a local hero and as a consequence was five times made mayor of the town. Appealing as this was to Kingsley's ideas of heroism, he was equally intrigued by the evident pride of the man who, some years later, unveiled 'a large monument to himself' saying that during the cholera epidemic of 1832, he had been 'intrepid and devoted in his attendance on the sufferers'.[27] Here, indeed, was a Carlylean hero who needed, fictionally at least, to be raised to Pauline humility.

But the strongest influence on Kingsley's delineation of Tom was probably Sir Henry Acland, whose work in Oxford is similar at several points to Tom's in Aberalva. Allusion has already been made to the parsimony of the Guardians in both instances, but it is significant for Kingsley's novel that Dr. Pusey 'placed the kitchen of Christ Church' at Dr. Acland's disposal; while Charles Marriott, the 'saintly friend both of Newman and of Pusey' worked untiringly throughout the Oxford epidemic in the selfless spirit in which Kingsley portrays Frank Headley. A parallel with Grace Harvey is also provided, not only by 'Oxford's anonymous Florence Nightingale' but also by Miss Felicia Skene, who rendered 'invaluable assistance', not only to Dr. Acland and his patients, but to all who were engaged on their behalf.[28] Like Florence Nightingale, she had wished to serve in the Crimea, but having been refused permission by the authorities, she assisted the doctor with his *Memoir*.

Both a 'saint and a heroine', Grace Harvey's is an ideal portrait, yet Kingsley loses no time in making her a reality. Unconvincing as she may be to modern readers, she was undoubtedly identified by Kingsley's generation with Grace Darling (1815–42), who lived at the Longstone lighthouse with her father. She had won national fame when, on the morning of 7 September, 1838, she and her father had rowed out from their lonely lighthouse in the Farne Islands and, by combined 'daring, strength, and skill', had managed to rescue four men and a woman from the luxury steamship *Forfarshire*, which had struck on a rock. Had she been a modern American, Kingsley tells us, Grace might well have been a 'lucrative medium'; while, as a mediaeval Catholic, she would certainly have been canonized. At a crucial point in the story Tom finds her telling a dying girl the legend of St. Dorothea, herself a model of that saint, since owing to her 'a new heart' grows up within him and her God becomes his (Ch. xiv, 227).

As Tom's dominant characteristic is cleverness, hers is goodness: 'Goodness rather than talent has given her wisdom, and goodness rather than courage, a power of using that wisdom'. Her intense imagination enables her 'to feel every bodily suffering . . . as acutely as the sufferer's self', and in her Christ-like capacity for sympathy lies her influence with the townsfolk: she bears 'the sins of all the parish'. A necessary complement to Tom's manliness, her goodness accords well with Kingsley's philosophy of woman. In the Christian context of the novel, womanly sympathy and tenderness as expressed in practice by women like Florence Nightingale and Felicia Skene lend a beauty and holiness to the art of amelioration that in Kingsley's view lay quite beyond the nature of man: 'Ah, woman, if you only knew how you carry our hearts in your hands, . . . what angels you might make of us all', (Ch. xi, 191) he cried in a moment of adulation; and Grace is depicted in this ideal perfection, although his obsession with 'duty' and 'goodness' indicate a Victorian idiom generally unappreciated today.

By comparison with Tom, Frank Headley is a minor character but his role, though similar to that of Luke in *Yeast* and of George in *Alton Locke*, is on a higher level than either of theirs and is correspondingly more important. Frank is a strong character, and altogether a man of principle and integrity. If Kingsley left an impression of prejudice against Catholic and High-church clergymen in *Yeast*, his portrait here belies that impression. Though Frank's Puseyism is shown to savour too much of 'system', he learns with the help of Tom and Grace to concern himself less with means than ends, and in the best Christian social manner he modifies it to meet the needs of his parish. During the epidemic his nobleness and devotion win the admiration of all and in surrendering formalism to service he finds his true vocation (Ch. XVII, 312).

The scene in which he and Grace share old Captain Willis's last Eucharist is strongly drawn. As Tom looks on from without and is softened in spite of himself, it becomes one of the touching moments in the book. Structurally, it also marks a step in Tom's conversion, a sequence in which no other High-churchman has been permitted to share.

Though *Two Years Ago* is a sermon, like Kingsley's other novels, the expository preacher allows the dramatic author increasing freedom to make the behaviour of his characters do his preaching for him. Since actions speak more loudly than words Kingsley dramatizes God's government of the world by showing character response to that government in relation to his circumstances. Each is a free agent and his mode of response shows his 'being' and shapes his 'doing'. Thus the circumstances in the life of a character become 'the alphabet of a divine language' illuminating conduct. Character is revealed, either as rising above and controlling circumstances, or as succumbing to them, and is accordingly either heroic or unheroic.

Elsley Vavasour is a weak character, but his role in the novel is exceeded in importance only by that of Tom Thurnall. The two youths are introduced at the beginning of the novel as divergent types, and as they go their separate ways they appear less as reconcilable opposites than as irreconcilable contraries. When they return to Whitbury briefly four years later, appearances are confirmed. As Tom Thurnall is heroic, John Briggs *alias* Elsley

Vavasour, is unheroic. The anti-hero is choleric and moody, discontented and humourless. Since, at Penalva Court he is effeminate, the youth is father to the man. He neglects his wife and children but, characteristically, is jealous of Major Campbell. He is also afraid of Tom, who knows his secret. When the cholera comes he does not remain to help, but accompanies his wife to Beddgelert in the foothills of Snowdon, where she has been sent for her safety; and when the epidemic is past and they are joined by Tom and his friends, who need a holiday before going to the Crimea, Elsley, still totally immersed in himself, has no thought of going with them to serve Queen and country. Moral courage is unknown to him (Ch. XIX, 343).

As the man, so the poet. An author of considerable genius, Elsley in his better moments has imparted the vision of a nobler life; and his earlier poems, Kingsley admits in a long authorial commentary on his character, stimulate a love for moral and physical beauty. Elsley has therefore 'fulfilled the proper function of the poet'. But as he allows his imagination 'to run riot' (Ch. XXIV, 408), he grows more vain and self-indulgent, more irritable and self-centred, so that his later poems are little more than mere 'word-painting'. As he shuts himself away from the world and abandons his interest in the vital concerns of mankind his poetry correspondingly declines.

Kingsley was apparently applying the familiar Coleridgean distinction between imagination and fancy, between those creations flowing from the 'living educts of the imagination' and those of fanciful association.[29] Though Elsley's 'sacred spark [is] fast dying out', largely because of his failing moral vigour, Kingsley's principal castigation of him as a poet lies in his evident loss of humanity. He has no interest in men as men. Though never blest with much love for mankind, he has 'transferred what sympathy he had left from needle-women and ragged schools, dwellers in Jacob's Island and sleepers in the dry arches of Waterloo Bridge, to sufferers of a more poetic class' – those of Italy and Greece (Ch. X, 151).

Elsley may represent, if not Byron, at least that most unheroic of men, the Byronic hero. Like Byron, Elsley arrogantly attempts to spurn the society that refuses to flatter his vanity. His voluntary isolation of Glyder Vawr is revealing and the author records thoughts of him that suggest the self-centred egotism of a diseased imagination:

He was a Prometheus on the peak of Caucasus, hurling defiance at the unjust Jove! His hopes, his love, his very honour – curse it! – ruined! Let the lightning stroke come! He were a coward to shrink from it. Let him face the worst unprotected, bare-headed, naked, and do battle himself, and nothing but himself, against the universe (Ch. xxi, 380).

Himself against the universe! Heroic as this may sound, it is the cry of a coward who, though fleeing from life, cannot escape himself. Like Childe Harold, he imagines that

> He who ascends to mountain-tops, shall find
> The loftiest peaks most wrapt in clouds and snow;

that

> He who surpasses or subdues mankind
> Must look down on the hate of those below.

As for him, 'against the universe' indeed,

> Though high *above* the sun of glory glow,
> And far *beneath* the earth and ocean spread,
> *Round* him are icy rocks, and loudly blow
> Contending tempests on his naked head,
> And thus reward the toil which to those summits led
>   (Canto III, xlv).

To this pretended superiority and exclusiveness Shakespeare and Milton have never subscribed. Loving human-kind and in return beloved by it, they shine as literary heroes in the firmament where 'the sun of glory glows'. Having abandoned even his 'word-painting', Elsley, immediately after this Promethean but empty show of strength, sinks 'upon the top of the cairn' into 'a dreamless sleep' until he is rescued by the hearty Cambridge boating-men, Wynd and Naylor.

Isolation turns men in upon themselves, and as it brings on Tom's, so it brings on Elsley's crisis. Brought face to face with himself, Tom, forgetting himself, rises from physical into spiritual heroism. In a similar situation, Elsley can only pity himself as an aggrieved party, curse an allegedly unappreciative mankind and a cruel nature, and sink unheroically into ignominious oblivion.

Kingsley leaves no doubt about this contrast. In August 1856 he, Tom Hughes, and Tom Taylor, went on a walking tour of Snowdonia. They concentrated on the country 'from Aber and Bangor north to Port Madoc and Festiniog'. Having thus surveyed 'every yard' of the ground, Kingsley turns the expedition to account in *Two Years Ago*. Moreover, 'the vision of Snowdon towering and wet against the background of blue flame, appearing and disappearing every moment' had come, he explained, from Froude, 'who lived there three years, saw it, and detailed it carefully, begging [him] to put it in'.[30] The description is therefore intensely realistic. In Chapter XXI, the 'melodrama' lies in Elsley, whose response to nature is as bathetic as his attitude to his circumstances, which are largely of his own making. Kingsley emphasizes this by bringing in Wynd and Naylor who, in the chase for Elsley, find his imagined horrors to be 'capital fun'. Kingsley would never have taken Elsley to Snowdon if he had not taken them there as well, 'as a wholesome foil to his madness'.[31]

Apparently taken up because Harriet Beecher Stowe and W. H. Hurlbert were severally visiting at Eversley during the autumn of 1856, the slavery theme was 'altogether an afterthought'. *Uncle Tom's Cabin* was at the height of its popularity while Hurlbert, who was also concerned with the abolitionist movement, becomes Stangrave in *Two Years Ago*.[32] To have interwoven the theme properly, Marie La Cordifiamma ought to have been brought under Grace Harvey's influence just as Stangrave and the other major characters are brought under Tom's. In this way, the parallelism between Tom and Grace would have extended to Stangrave and thus unified the plot and knit the themes compactly together.

Kingsley could not omit a theme so vitally contemporary and so gratuitously given (Ch. XIV, 236). Slavery provided a golden opportunity to preach the essential brotherhood of man while strengthening the cholera theme, and his attitudes to colour and social discrimination as expressed in the novel are substantially those in his third sermon on cholera:

God made of one blood all nations to dwell on the face of the earth. The same food will feed us all alike. The same cholera will kill us all alike. And we can give the cholera to each other; we can give each other the infection, not merely by our touch and breath, for diseased beasts can do that, but by housing our families and our tenants badly. This is the secret of the innocent suffering for the guilty, in pestilences, and famines, and disorders, which are handed down from father to child, that we are all of the same blood.[33]

The delineation of Stangrave as unheroic supports the anti-hero theme detailed in Vavasour's story, and advances Kingsley's greater theme of kingdom-building as necessarily the work of heroes. Marie has been rescued from slavery by Tom's disinterested heroism, but Stangrave, though in love with her, thinks he can do nothing for her or for her people. Freedom is their right, however, and Kingsley cannot resist a further opportunity to preach:

Heroic souls in old times had no more opportunities than we have: but they used them. There were daring deeds to be done then – are there none now? Sacrifices to be made – are there none now? Wrongs to be redressed – are there none now? Let anyone set his heart, in these days, to do what is right [Marie tells Stangrave], . . .; and it will not be long ere his brow is stamped with all that goes to make up the heroical expression – with noble indignation, noble self-restraint, great hopes, great sorrows; perhaps, even, with the print of the martyr's crown of thorns (Ch. VII, 113).

But Stangrave is no hero, nor does he pretend to be. The sleeping-partner in a great firm of wealthy New York merchants, he lives in a luxurious dream. Travelling the world over he dispassionately looks upon people and places while gathering treasures for his personal paradise – a Tennysonian Palace of Art. A liberty-loving American, he leaves every man to find his own way even as he is left to build his private kingdom. *Laissez-faire*, he thinks, is tolerant and democratic.

Only at the close of the novel with Marie's words ringing in his ears does he see that 'the story of the human race is the story of its heroes and martyrs', and that he, too, can be a hero. In the interests of what he once called toleration, he sat by, 'seeing the devil have it all his own way'. Now, in the name of justice, he must act. Honour calls, and his task is not in the Crimea but in America itself.

The cholera stemmed, the Aberalvan stage grows quiet as the

actors turn outward to the world. 'Life is meant for work, and not for ease; to labour in danger and in dread; to do a little good ere the night comes, when no man can work . . .' (Ch. XXII, 402). Selfless Christian practice derives from heroic duty in creating a better world:

> Be good, sweet maid, and let who will be clever;
> Do noble things, not dream them, all day long;
> And so make Life, Death, and that vast For Ever,
> One grand sweet song.

CHAPTER 8

Hereward the Wake

Ten years after publishing *Westward Ho !* Kingsley began serializing 'Hereward, the Last of the English'. In the January issue of *Good Words* (1865)[1] appeared the Prelude and Chapter I, and the story grew each month by three, four, or – more frequently – five chapters, and concluded in the December issue. The following year – eight hundred after the battle of Hastings – *Hereward the Wake*, emended, more amply documented than the serial and sub-titled 'Last of the English' appeared in two volumes, the cover of each bearing the arms of Wake, surmounted by the Wake knot in which 'two monks' girdles are worked into the form of the letter W' and inscribed beneath, *Vigila et Ora*. Watch is the word for the guardian of the army, but only in a solitary place can the suppliant pray, 'Except the Lord keep the city, the watchman waketh but in vain';[2] and this is the sum of Kingsley's last novel.

Hereward the Wake is a saga of Danish–Saxon England on the eve of the Norman Conquest. A coarse woodcut of the eleventh century, in black and white, and stained with the barbarous colours of a dark age, the book is a thrilling tale of adventure for teen-aged boys to whom battles and bloodshed are but incidentals in the seething excitement and turbulent surface action of a dauntless hero with whom they can readily identify. But it is also the portrait of a civilization in the last phase of its life, epic in scope, and more nearly history than fiction. Yet, because it is a legend subdued by the grey mists of a haunted and far distant past, it becomes high romance and conveys an air of fabulous unreality.

The scene is set in the East Anglian fenland. Occupying the drainage basin of the rivers Witham, Welland, Nene, and Great Ouse, it comprises half a million acres lying west and south of the Wash, extending more than seventy miles in length from Lincoln to Cambridge, and approximately thirty-five in breadth from Stamford to Brandon. As Kingsley's story draws to a close, Richard de Rulos, who has married Hereward's granddaughter and has therefore succeeded to the Lordship of Bourne and Deeping, begins in the twelfth century to enclose and drain the Deeping fen, and although the work continued intermittently during succeeding centuries, complete reclamation was accomplished only in Kingsley's life-time.

In Hereward's day the fens were utterly undrained,

dark and noisome, heavy with the wings of wildfowl, clouded in winter by fog and snow, stinking in summer with marsh gas, and inhabited by a wild, amphibious race of savages, fishers, and fowlers, robbers and murderers, who paddled from reedy isle to quaking reed-beds. . . .[3]

Primeval, wild, and chaotic, the whole area was a dismal and mysterious swamp. So inaccessible was Ely, the largest of the fen islands that, at the time of the Conquest, Hereward and 'the last of the English' took refuge there from their enemy, and for two years spiritedly defied their Norman tyrants.[4]

But when Kingsley was a boy the fens were much less formidable than they had been in Hereward's dark time. Although the Kingsley family left Barnack when Charles was eleven, he had never forgotten 'the shining meres, the golden reed-beds', the innumerable water-fowl, gaudy insects, and wild nature that throve there. As a boy he had often accompanied his father on hunting expeditions, when the sweep of flat fenland scenery was stamped on his impressionable mind, and he has described it at length in *Prose Idylls*,[5] and *Hereward*.[6] He had always cherished the panoramic vistas that took in the green flats stretching away to a far horizon where, from the curve of the earth, 'the distant trees and islands were hulled down like ships at sea'.

During his undergraduate days at Cambridge he had spent many an idle afternoon punting in their teeming fastnesses and, always saw them with the wonder of childhood, a state more readily identifiable with that of the primeval wildness eight hundred years before when Hereward had startled great flocks of fowl with his war-cry, "A Wake! A Wake!", as they rose and encircled his helmeted head.[7]

In 1848, that crucial year in which Kingsley was aflame with *Politics for the People*, *Yeast*, and *Alton Locke*, he and Maurice spent 'three priceless days' in the fen country. At the close of the first volume of *Hereward* the hero and his mother row to Crowland Abbey, where she will 'see nought but English faces, hear English chants, and die a free Englishwoman under St. Guthlac's wings' (Ch. xix); and eight hundred years later in the peaceful ruin of that ancient retreat Maurice taught Kingsley 'more than [he] could tell'.[8] We shall never know the extent to which Kingsley was indebted to his mentor for *Hereward*, but it is safe to assume that his bright picture of life in the eleventh century was embellished with Maurice's views of that society, of its contribution to history, and of both brought forward from that remote age to 1848.

The Saint's Tragedy had been in print but six months and Baron Bunsen had suggested that Kingsley might continue Shakespeare's historical plays.[9] The research for St. Elizabeth of Hungary had given him insight into the Middle Ages, and at Crowland with Maurice murmuring in his ear, the world of 1066 struck him with peculiar force. He planned to write another play, a hero's tragedy this time rather than a saint's, but *Hypatia* and *Westward Ho!* intervened so that, when Kingsley finally got round to it, he made *Hereward* into a novel as well, although the structure of it has much in common with Shakespearean tragedy and draws parallels with *Antony and Cleopatra.*

The years between *Westward Ho!* and *Hereward* were crowded with literary activity. After the Elizabethan novel and *Glaucus,* had come *The Heroes* (1856) and, the following year, *Two Years Ago.* With the exception of 1862 at least one title came out each year, and while he was sending instalments of 'Hereward' to *Good Words* he wrote the usual sermons and prepared a special series on David. Feeling that a 'new era' had dawned after his appointment to the Regius professorship of Modern History at Cambridge on 9 May, 1860, and, within a twelvemonth, to the 'honour and duty' of instructing the Prince of Wales, he had thought 'all that book-writing was over'. But he soon found the preparation of lectures to be more onerous than 'book-writing' and, for him, far less congenial. The burden became almost insupportable, and as if to remind him of the vanity of life, the decade saw an unusually large number of deaths, which had a sobering effect on him. Prince

Albert's passing in 1861 touched him deeply, while the loss of his old King's College friend, John Parker, who had shared his enthusiasm for reform and had published *Yeast*, left him with the feeling, less that a new era was opening than that a chapter in his life had closed. *Hereward the Wake* thus belongs to Kingsley's later career.

Because his lectures drew fire from academia, he felt driven to more intensive research and he told the Master of Trinity that, by the time he had prepared and delivered a term's lectures, he was 'half-witted'. His unfortunate controversy with Cardinal Newman broke in 1864 and the misunderstanding added a further strain. Friends dissuaded him from resigning, but by midsummer he was 'broken in strength', forbidden to preach, and ordered to take a three months' rest. It had not come a moment too soon, and the whole family settled 'quietly' not, as was Kingsley's wont, in the West Country, but 'on the coast of Norfolk'.

Kingsley was actually writing *Hereward*, then, when he made his last visit to the fens. Indeed, the pattern of the submissions to *Good Words* suggests that Kingsley's arrival in the fenland was coincident with the return, in the tale, of Hereward from Flanders. The June instalment ends with the account of Hereward's sailing for England (Ch. XXII), while the July contribution begins with his recruiting activities. On the Norfolk coast Kingsley was in the locale of his story and, at the same time, within easy reach of libraries, both in Cambridge, and in Peterborough Cathedral, where his sources were to be found.

The chroniclers are inconsistent in their accounts of Hereward, and his genuine history is therefore scanty. For the period itself, Kingsley appears to have relied on Francis Palgrave's *History of the Anglo-Saxons*, and for Hereward's history, on E. A. Freeman's *History of the Norman Conquest*.[10] Taking only a part of the time treated in the *History*, *William the Conqueror*[11] concentrates on William, and shows him in juxtaposition with Hereward, whose brief history it summarizes. Admitting the difficulty of disentangling the few details of his real history from the legendary accounts, Freeman declares Hereward's descent and birth-place to be un-uncertain, but writes that

he was assuredly a man of Lincolnshire, and assuredly not the son of
Earl Leofric. For some unknown cause, he had been banished in the days
of Edward or of Harold. He now came back to lead his countrymen
against William. He was the soul of the movement of which the abbey
of Ely became the centre.

Freeman also elaborates on the activities of the Danish sympathizers
who joined Hereward and assisted him in his defiance of William:

The isle, then easily defensible, was the last English ground on which
the Conqueror was defied by Englishmen fighting for England. The
men of the Fenland were zealous; the monks of Ely were zealous;
helpers came in from other parts of England. English leaders left their
shelter in Scotland to share the dangers of their countrymen; even
Edwin and Morkere at last plucked up heart to leave William's court and
join the patriotic movement. Edwin was pursued; he was betrayed by
traitors; he was overtaken and slain, to William's deep grief, we are
told. His brother reached the isle, and helped in its defence.

With equal brevity, while recognizing divergent accounts, Freeman
states the outcome:

The isle was stoutly attacked and stoutly defended, till, according to one
version, the monks betrayed the stronghold to the King. According
to another, Morkere was induced to surrender by promises of mercy
which William failed to fulfil. In any case, before the year 1071 was
ended, the isle of Ely was in William's hands. Hereward alone with a
few companions made their way out to sea.

Freeman's concluding remarks drift from history into legend, which
speaks of Hereward

as admitted to William's peace and favour. One makes him die quietly,
another kills him at the hands of Norman enemies, but not at William's
bidding or with William's knowledge. Evidence a little better suggests
that he bore arms for his new sovereign beyond the sea. . . .

On this slight narrative Kingsley built *Hereward the Wake*.
Whereas history leaves Hereward's descent and birth-place un-
certain, Kingsley boldly makes him a son of Earl Leofric Lord of
Bourne, and Lady Godiva. Whereas history speaks of banishment
for an unknown reason, Kingsley's hero is outlawed by King Edward
the Confessor at their request, and their reasons are clearly stated.
At eighteen, Hereward, though golden-haired and handsome, is

wild and swaggering, 'the bully and the ruffian of all the fens'. He is simply unmanageable. He disobeys his father and abuses the local tenantry. As Kingsley's story begins, he has just manhandled Herluin, the Norman steward of Peterborough Abbey, and taken the good man's money; and according to his mother and the superstition of the time, this escapade renders him 'godless', putting him beyond the pale of civilized Christian society. To rob a monk was to rob, not merely a holy Father and the Abbey of Peterborough, but St. Peter himself, whose displeasure must henceforth endanger the whole Church (Ch. 1, 46). Banishment was the only remedy, and Hereward lets himself be outlawed 'like a true hero'.

Whereas Freeman offers a choice in the betrayers of Ely, Kingsley freely assigns the deed to the monks, who were either Norman infiltrators into the English Church, or English monks with Norman sympathies. Again, Freeman suggests three alternatives for the account of Hereward's end, whereas Kingsley accepts that which 'kills him at the hands of Norman enemies'. In every case the novelist chooses the alternative that is most dramatic, always pitting Englishmen against alien and invading Normans. History has nothing to say about the women in Hereward's life, whether concerning the craven part played by Alftruda, or the devoted self-sacrifice of Torfrida; nor is there anything, lastly, about the life of Hereward's gang in the greenwood.

Kingsley clothes these meagre facts, and colours Hereward's scanty history. In his hands the action begins, the major characters come alive, tensions arise, and an Old-English atmosphere is created. Living human beings come upon the stage and the narrative engenders excitement and suspense. A great house is divided against itself when harsh discipline displaces familial love; but another kind of devotion is shown when Martin Lightfoot accompanies the young renegade into the world.

Kingsley followed additional 'facts' as 'strictly' as he could, 'altering none which [he] found, and inventing little more than was needed to give the story coherence'. The undoubted and original authorities for Hereward's history are, besides the passages in Domesday referred to by Freeman and quoted by Kingsley, the Anglo-Saxon Chronicle for the years 1070–1, Florence of Worcester,

Hugh Candidus, William of Malmesbury, and other chroniclers, including Ordericus Vitalis.[12] Kingsley also extensively used the *Liber Eliensis*, the chronicle of Ely, compiled by certain monks and edited by D. J. Stewart;[13] and a 'fragment', which is evidently the *De Gestis Herewardi* presumed to be by Richard of Ely.

Though Kingsley consulted these, he recognized his main sources, both authentic and legendary, in a note in the January issue of *Good Words* (1865):

The story of Hereward (often sung by minstrels and old wives in succeeding generations) may be found in the *Metrical Chronicle of Geoffrey Gaimar*, and in the prose *Life of Hereward* (paraphrased from that written by Leofric, his house-priest), and in the valuable fragment *Of the Family of Hereward*. These have all three been edited by Mr. T. Wright. The account of Hereward in Ingulf seems taken, and that carelessly, from the same source as the Latin prose, *De Gestis Herewardi*. A few curious details may be found in Peter of Blois' continuation of Ingulf; and more, concerning the sack of Peterborough, in the Anglo-Saxon Chronicle.

He particularly specifies Geoffrey Gaimar's *Estoire des Engles*[14] edited by Thomas Wright for the Caxton Society, as the Latin work to which he was most indebted. It is illustrated with notes and an appendix containing, among other biographies,[15] the Life of Hereward. Wright's edition was based on that of Francisque Michel's *Chroniques Anglo-Normandes* (1839), which he had edited from transcripts in the library at Trinity College. But he also did a vigorous English version based on his edited Latin edition and, although he took his account of Hereward's death from Gaimar, his history of Hereward is otherwise taken 'almost literally' from *Gesta Herewardi Saxoni* (preserved in a manuscript of the twelfth century), which he compared with other chronicles of the time; and this work Kingsley has followed most closely as printed first, in *Ainsworth's Magazine* (May, 1845) and later, in Wright's *Essays* (1846).[16] Wright had 'disinterred' Hereward, and had taught Kingsley 'how to furbish his [hero's] rusty harness, botch his bursten saddle and send him forth once more, upon the ghost of his gallant mare'. He also read the proofs of *Hereward*, and Kingsley recognized his debt to him in a dedicatory letter following the title-page of the novel. Wright's brief account had acted on his imagination in much the same way as Maurice's sermons had done and Kingsley's story, expanded with intimate details and glowing descriptions in his flowing style, utterly eclipses Wright's.

Kingsley's method in *Hereward* resembles that in *Westward Ho!*. He uses 'historical characters and events as the chief element in the story', and imaginary characters as the machinery needed to carry on the action. While the use of history seems different in *Hereward*, it really is not. Because some parts of the hero's life have been transmitted through minstrelsy and popular songs, which were compiled and woven into a poetic narrative early in the twelfth century, Hereward, though an actual historical personage, takes on the attributes of an imaginary character. In *Westward Ho!*, Amyas Leigh, though an imaginary hero, shares much with Francis Drake, an historical personage. Yet each remains distinct. In *Hereward the Wake* the hero is at one and the same time historical and imaginary.

Wright's legendary and poetic tales, then, were valuable to Kingsley. Though they were only half-truths, Kingsley saw that he need not hesitate to use them in presenting the whole as 'a true picture of the struggle between the last of the Saxon heroes and the oppressors of his country'.[17] The 'poetry of history' may misrepresent 'the actions but not the character of its hero', and it undoubtedly gives us 'a true picture . . . of the character of his age' as well. Kingsley had only to bring his imagination and creative genius to the subject to make the mass of material his own, and while he adhered to the history as researched by Freeman and others, he diverted the poetry of that history to the creation of a highly imaginative work of art and *Hereward the Wake* is authentically historical within its terms of reference.

Hereward's history dictated its own sequence, and conflicting attributes in the hero's personality complicated the structure. The familiar steps in religious conversion, which Kingsley always used as a framework, are not wanting in this, but they are less suitable here than in the other novels, as we shall see. The Biblical record of the conversion of Israel expresses alternating turnings to and from God, thus forming a 'perpetual systole and diastole' of the nation, and though not overt in Hereward, the opposing movements are vital to the structure of the novel. This is clearly indicated by

Kingsley's division of the serial into two volumes, ending the first with the eviction of the Normans from Bourne, and beginning the second with Hereward's knighthood.

The first volume (Ch. I–XIX) introduces the 'godless and god-forgotten' Hereward who, in the course of his wanderings from court to court, performs noble and heroic deeds. That each of them succours the weak seems incidental. That each demands ever greater courage and skill as the hero moves onward, is not. It is therefore fitting that the first volume should end with Hereward's climactic annihilation of the Normans at Bourne. That he success-fully executes deed after deed suggests, on the physical side, the twelve labours of the Herculean hero,[18] and on the ethical, a gradual ascent in chivalry and godliness. The obliteration of the Normans from Bourne symbolizes alike, the emergence of the full-blown hero and his acceptance of an epic mission to drive the Norman invaders from England, and the first volume may therefore be regarded as a systolic movement of the familiar conversion process.

The second volume (Ch. XX–XLII) opens with Hereward's knighthood. As the hero has grown in strength and magnificence, so he has added all the ethical qualities required for the belt of the true, gentle, and perfect knight. In spite of his heroism and prowess, however, his knightly qualities are soon seen to be dubious and tentative since, as this volume progresses his chivalry wanes and he gradually sinks into ruffianism, renewed outlawry, and shame, so that the movement here is the reverse of that in the first volume. Just as his prowess at Bourne symbolizes the redemption of England and the defeat of the Normans, so now his personal shortcomings, which augur his ultimate fall, prognosticate the degradation and fall of England. In terms of religious conversion, then, the second volume of *Hereward* records a diastolic defection in both theme and structure.

That a personable earl's son should be wild and unmanageable is natural enough. That he should be thrust upon the world and chastened in the harsh school of experience is good, and that his better self should conquer and manifest itself in appropriate action as he grows in wisdom and stature is better still. That he should achieve the excellence of knightly chivalry is best of all. 'I hold', says Hereward in his moment of greatness, 'that it is nobler to receive sword and belt from a man of God, than from a man of blood like one's self; for the fittest man to consecrate the soldier of an earthly king, is the soldier of Christ the King of kings'.[19] But to fall from knighthood into shame and guilty conscience is a tragedy, and *Hereward the Wake* is a tragedy.

Regarded as drama, the first six chapters of the book may be seen as constituting the first act, with Hereward's further adventures in Flanders and his courtship of Torfrida as covering the second. The third act, which in tragedy usually includes the structural climax, must then cover those chapters which focus the attention on England, namely, those from Chapter XVII, which brings Hereward the news of Stamford Bridge and Hastings, on through to the conclusion of the sack of Peterborough in Chapter XXVI. If these are accepted as the third act, the dramatic climax (Ch. XX) then falls in the middle, both of the act itself, and of the whole novel and, at the same time, retains the sack, a vital episode in the drama, in a central position. The defence of Ely then becomes a fourth act (Ch. XXVII–XXXIII), while the fifth and last includes the closing chapters, the scenes of which are laid in the Bruneswald, with the magnificent dramatic climactic scene at Bourne.

The incidents contributing to the rising action occur in the episodic fables recounted chapter after chapter, and scene after scene, in Hereward's progress. In all of these episodes the emphasis is placed on strength and sheer muscle-flexing, with little thought of anything beyond the practical business of demolishing the opponent, but the hero's courage, strength, and bravery, all contribute to the rising action.

But progress towards knighthood demands a corresponding development in ethical qualities, a growth in godliness, and this task is assigned to Torfrida. In what may be termed the second act, the ethical aspect of the rising action unfolds under her guidance. When a stranger comes riding into St. Omer and begins to perform his 'doughty deeds' her curiosity is aroused; and when a mailed knight appears, Torfrida recognizes him as Hereward come hot from the tournament with her favour, which he has won from Sir Ascelin, and which she impulsively binds round his helm. 'Wear it before all the world', she cries, 'and guard it as you only can'. With his usual impetuosity, the rough wooer in turn swears by the cross round her neck: 'You only I will love, and you I will love in all honesty, before all the angels of heaven. . . .', he declares; and he turns immediately to further feats of strength in the service of the Count.

During their brief courtship (Ch. XII) Torfrida is often pained by Hereward's rude manners, but she sets herself 'to teach and train the wild outlaw into her ideal of a very perfect knight'. She talks to him of

modesty and humility, the root of all virtues; of chivalry and self-sacrifice; of respect to the weak, and mercy to the fallen; of devotion to God, and awe of His commandments. She [sets] before him the example of ancient heroes and philosophers, of saints and martyrs; and as much [awes] him by her learning, as by the new world of higher and purer morality, which [is] opened for the first time to the wandering Viking.[20]

Torfrida thus raises him to the 'courtesy' of the knight. Mental and physical strengths develop together, and the changing hero improves as he moves forward along the road to knighthood.

Learning of the national calamities at Stamford Bridge and Hastings, he becomes aware of his duty and, repenting his misspent youth, he is now full of patriotic zeal and determined to redeem England for the descendants of Canute. The timely arrival of Countess Gyda, the distraught mother of the slain Harold, convinces him of his destiny and his investigatory visit to England in 1068 signifies the beginning of his mission, which supplies the culminating episodes in the rising action.

The slaughter of the carousing Normans in his father's hall avenges the death of his brother, but the act also signifies the last and most difficult of the numerous feats of physical skill necessary to be accomplished before knighthood. Then, reconciled with his mother, he is filled with humility, 'the root of all virtues', and kindly escorts the now broken Godiva to Crowland. In this proud moment he combines physical with spiritual maturity, for 'there he knelt, and vowed a vow to God and St. Guthlac and the Lady Torfrida, his true love, never to leave from slaying while there was a Frenchman left alive on English ground'.[21] This is swiftly followed by a warning to Prior Herluin that the abbey itself will not be spared if the monks attempt to install the Norman Thorold as the successor of his uncle, Abbot Brand. Knighted and 'a new man', he returns to Bourne, accepts the leadership of the army, promises to drive the French back into Normandy, unite Saxons with Danes, and restore the Danish line to the throne of a free and independent England. At last the powerful, courageous, and brave Hereward has surrendered to the chivalric service of the weak in the epic interests of his country.

The knighting ceremony is the pinnacle of the climax. As such, however, it marks at one and the same time the end of the rising action in the tragic plot and the beginning of the *dénouement*. On the point of receiving the accolade, he is a veritable champion of England and English monks, a hero, and 'a very perfect knight':

I am a very foolish, vain, sinful man, who have come through great adventures, I know not how, to great and strange happiness; and now again to great and strange sorrows; and to an adventure greater and stranger than all that has befallen me from my youth up until now. Therefore make me not proud [he pleads], but keep me modest and lowly, as befits all true knights and penitent sinners: for they tell me that God resists the proud, and giveth grace to the humble. And I have that to do which do I cannot, unless God and His saints give me grace from this day forth.[22]

Knighted, he promises to use his sword for the 'punishment of evil doers', for the 'defence' of women and orphans, the poor and the oppressed, and the monks as 'the servants of God'.

The dramatic climax of the novel occurs in his choice of a motto to match the Wake knot he has selected to replace the bear in his arms. *Vigila et Ora*, suggests the good monk. 'Watch and pray', says Hereward 'half sadly'. 'I will watch, and my wife shall pray', he adds, 'and so will the work be well parted between us'.[23] In this moment of solemn dedication he is not wholly 'a man of God'. Of watchfulness and undaunted action he is sure. But the humility and magnanimity that have brought him to knighthood are but half his, mere props supplied by another and likely to be cast aside like the magic armour Torfrida had given him. Like his age, Hereward is half Christian, half pagan, and this makes it difficult convincingly to convey the Christian socialism that Kingsley would preach. Hereward's inadequacy is a sad prognostication of evils to come, and they come at once.

No sooner has Hereward taken back his sword 'in the name of God' than, a very David, he sallies forth to meet his Goliath, one favouring the French. Brute strength has immediately gained an ascendancy over humility. Other signs are not wanting that the *dénouement* has begun. Returning from Flanders, Hereward disagrees with Asbiorn, and the forces sent by King Sweyn of Denmark are thus squandered. Indicative of the dissension, not only between Saxons and Danes, but among the Danish earls themselves, the discord among William's enemies gives him needed time, and he ruthlessly quells the Danish forces. Hereward is now forced to recognize William's wisdom, which Torfrida, whose sorcery is rumoured to be the source of his power, had not been able to do: 'Hereward, Hereward, have I not told you, though body be strong, mind is stronger'[24]

Nor does Hereward cover himself with glory in the sack of Peterborough (Ch. XXVI). As the last stand of the English against the French, the offensive ought to have been impressive. Instead it is marked with desecration and futility. King Sweyn with 'a mighty fleet' sweeps up the Ouse towards Ely, and Asbiorn with another moves up the Nene. 'All the chivalry of Denmark and Ireland' is come, but with it come also

– Vikings from Jomsburg and Arkona, Gottlanders from Wisby; and with them their heathen tributaries, Wends, Finns, Esthonians, Courlanders, Russians from Novogorod and the heart of Holmgard, Letts who still offered, in the forest of Rugen, human victims to four-headed Swantowit. . . .[25]

The motley crowd bodes ill for the engagement. Hereward sanctions the sacking of Peterborough and, dubbed knight in that very church as Herluin reminds him, he is torn between the French, and 'a smaller faction of stout-hearted English' who deserve his protection. But the old berserker spirit rises and since the Danes have to be paid, they, rather than the French, had better have 'St. Peter's gold'. The mob sweep into the abbey past Herluin, who is holding the crucifix high above their heads, and rush to the treasure. The theft for which Hereward had been outlawed thirty years earlier is now rapacity on a national scale. Recking of nothing, they go into the monastery. They

clomb up to the holy rood, then took the crown from our Lord's head, all of beaten gold; then took the 'foot-spur' that was underneath his foot, which was all of red gold. They clomb up to the steeple, brought down the crosier that was there hidden; it was of gold and of silver. They took there two golden shrines, and nine of silver; and they took fifteen great roods, both of gold and of silver. They took there so much gold and silver, and so many treasures in money, and in raiment, and in books, as no man may tell to another, saying that they did it from affection to the monastery.[26]

Though Hereward invites the 'wolves and ravens' to 'eat gold, drink gold, roll in gold', his own 'treasure' is of a different kind. He rescues the ladies, and finds Alftruda, now 'far more beautiful than Torfrida', and very wealthy. Ready to leave her first husband, she appeals to his pride and, in rescuing her, he has rescued the 'villain', a viper for his bosom. He has assured his own fall and, incidentally as it were, that of England as well.

It is unnecessary to elaborate on the *dénouement*. King Sweyn berates himself for having come too late: 'While William the Frenchman is king by the sword, and Edgar the Englishman king by proclamation of Earls and Thanes, there seems no room . . . for Sweyn, nephew of Canute, king of kings'.[27]

The hero grows incapable of co-operation. Pride and brute strength govern as he waxes increasingly capricious. The carnage that follows his loss of temper in the king's court is reckless and unworthy, the desperate performance of one gone berserk, whose honour, like Antony's, is gone but who, unlike Antony, knows not that he has lost himself.[28]

Kingsley requires two further indications of his hero's approaching fall. He has forsaken his wife, the 'praying half' of himself and has thus abandoned chivalry and honour. But only the loss of sword Brainbiter, which he associates with brute strength, informs him that 'his luck [has] turned'.[29] Next, Torfrida confesses to the practice of sorcery, not because it is true, for she has 'long since abandoned these frivolous vanities,[30] but because Kingsley must demonstrate her selflessness and at the same time allow his protagonist to accomplish his own fall. 'The Father of men seems . . . to have put before this splendid barbarian good and evil, saying Choose! And he knew that the evil was evil, and chose it nevertheless'.[31]

The scene in which Hereward is surrounded by his enemies comes as a relief. The spectacle of the magnificent hero falling from knighthood into knavery and ending at last as a churlish ruffian is agonizing, and the guilty flash of conscience that confronts him, not only with the faces of his killers, but with those he has wantonly killed, is a powerful nemesis. Kingsley has only to show him unarmed, but rising to defend himself with his old Herculean strength and unrivalled bravery as he is hewn down at last.

This analysis in terms of tragic drama clarifies Kingsley's conversional plan for his Christian social thesis, but we must remember that although it is inherent in the underlying structure of the novel, Kingsley clearly knew too much about Anglo-Danish history and culture to apply the same standards to Hereward as he had done to Raphael Aben-Ezra and Amyas Leigh. As suggested above, Hereward's is not a conversion in the full sense of the word because the hero is a representative of a world that, although Christian in name, is still barbarous and crude and still beset with superstitious paganism. While the sacking of Bourne and the knighthood may be regarded from a Christian view-point as the turning-point in the hero's tragedy, it is important to see that the sins marking Hereward's *dénouement* are but 'the sins of the age' (Ch. XLI, 496). Immediately after being knighted, he kills the Frenchman, Earl Warrenne's brother; he has just sworn to, and the monks in the half-pagan spirit of the age have approved his oath. The failure of the plan with King Sweyn's brother is put squarely on the latter's unaccommodating pride, and the King rebukes him for not obeying his orders. This, too, is the fault of the time. Hereward's only 'real sin', that cutting across both pagan and Christian standards of the time, was his falsehood to Torfrida; and this comes very late in the book, though the possibility of it is foreseen much earlier.

Plot is character, and Hereward's has largely emerged in the revelation of the tragic plot itself. Pride is the fundamental fault in the hero's nature. The fierce independence that stamps him as a leader is presented, first, simply as the mark of a strong-willed youth by whom, under channelled discipline, great things are done. Apart from Torfrida, however, no discipline is acceptable to him, and even she is cast aside. His arrogance is attributable to an insensitivity of self-idolatry, for like Napoleon and Hitler, Hereward is blinded by his own ego.

But Hereward, after all, is a 'splendid barbarian'. More pagan than Christian, he is magnificent in the context of his time. His very name proclaims him the guardian of the army and, like David of old, none 'touches the harp like him'. After he succours the Princess of Cornwall he bursts into Viking song, proudly advertising his undaunted ferocity and his championship of the weak; and at the meeting of the Anglo-Danish leaders, Sweyn Ulfsson declares that three such men as Hereward could have driven the Normans for ever from English soil. Kingsley waxes rhetorical as he proclaims (Ch. XLI) the spirit of Hereward to be the spirit of freedom, that which was to make England a great nation and, in the fullness of time, the progenitor of 'still greater nations in lands yet unknown'. Hereward is his genuinely muscular hero.

Hereward the Wake is a novel of Christian social purpose. Because Saxons rose against Danes and Danes opposed Saxons, the country was doomed: 'Hereward Leofricsson tells Harold Godwinsson that he is his equal, . . . that he will never put his hands between the hands of a son of Godwin'.[32] Not until the day that William is 'king of all England' will Hereward 'be his man'. Families are divided as brother rises against brother, and father against son, a pattern in the house of Hereward as in the king's, since Harold must slay his outlawed brother, Tosti, in an effort to secure his throne. The land of Saxon England has been accumulated in the hands of an aristocracy numerically small, and closely related in blood, 'a state of things', says Kingsley, 'sufficient in itself to account for the easy victory of the French'.[33] The old nobility of England is dying 'up and down the ruts and shaughs, like wounded birds'.[34]

Rugged individualism frustrates brotherhood. Because Waltheof's knights are all 'free gentlemen', 'every one of them must needs have his own way, and choose the best ground', and Hereward declares their resistance to have failed because there are a dozen men in England like himself, 'every man wanting his own way'.[35] Only his own fanatical independence prolongs the siege of Ely. It must fall at last, for he knows 'the indomitable persistence' and 'the boundless resources' of William, but yield he will not.[36] He cannot accept defeat though it destroy the race itself. 'Honour to the last heroes of the old English race',[37] but greater honour still to him who tempers his will with judgment and calm reason.

Though Saxon and Dane united in their dislike of the invading Norman, their animosities, jealousies, and bickerings opened the church door to the Norman monk. Here, at the core of old English civilization the canker grew and spread throughout the whole of their social fabric. As a Christian and social institution the Church before the Conquest grew more and more unsatisfactory. Though Crowland had been set apart as a place of refuge for penitents of every class and condition who kept the peace, the English Church increasingly fell under the political domination of the Papacy. Hildebrand was converting the 'mere ascendancy of the Holy See into actual sovereignty of the states of Christendom' and, as one of them, England had long been his object. To that end had the Norman monks come, defending their conquest as 'a mission for converting the savages', then representing them as 'almost heathen'. 'Popish as the English Church of the age was', wrote Kingsley, it was 'unfortunately for it, not popish enough; and from its insular freedom, obnoxious to the Church of Rome and the ultramontane clergy of Normandy'.[38] When Lanfranc succeeds the deposed Stigand as archbishop of Canterbury, he works closely with Hildebrand to support William's claim and subject the English Church.

Kingsley depicts the Church as superstitious and worldly, and immersed in political intrigue; and the monks prove most effective in dividing the kingdom. Hereward's outlawry stems from his quarrel with the Norman Herluin, whose injustice and cruelty fostered revenge. The richest abbey in England was sacked to prevent the hated Thorold from ruling the Golden Borough for William and the Pope. But Peterborough is burned, and the Church ultimately pays Hereward a high ransom for the Abbot's

release from the greenwood. Thorold is installed and Papal rapacity
proceeds apace. William wins the Ely monks by threatening to
confiscate their lands beyond the abbey precincts, 'large and of
great value'. Greed and superstition have made cowards of them and,
finally, traitors.[39]

Vital to Kingsley's story, the theme is essential for the sermon
on social ethics in the making of history. Romanism gets relatively
little attention in *Hereward*, but Kingsley's sentiments are in
accord with the testimony of Lord Lytton, who declares in *Harold*
that 'the heart of England never forgave that league of the Pope
with the Conqueror'.[40] He adds that 'the seeds of the Reformed
Religion were trampled deep into the Saxon soil by the feet of the
invading Norman'. Hereward was not the only man to resent the
secular arm of the Church. Lord Lytton's declaration puts Kingsley's
novel in perspective with *Hypatia* and *Westward Ho!* as representing
a decisive moment in the history of the English Church, half-way
between Cyril's monks in the fifth century and Queen Elizabeth's
'worthies' in the sixteenth.

After dealing in *Westward Ho!* with the greatest deliverance in
English history, Kingsley turned to the greatest defeat, the greatest
failure to be delivered. His conception of the workings of Providence
in history had to allow for both, for even national defeat reveals the
guiding hand of God. Hereward's sins – his desertion of Torfrida
excepted – are the sins of his age, and they alone effect the overthrow of the nation. In *Hereward* Kingsley thus authenticates the
justice and impartiality of Providence in His dealings with men and,
at the same time, he suggests that disobedience *sub specie aeternitatis*
has caused them to be confounded in their day and generation, that
succeeding ages may listen again to the voice of conscience and
resume once more their Godward tendency.

But Kingsley's severest social criticism in *Hereward* is reserved
for the individual, and for those in his own century who persisted
in misunderstanding his teaching on the ideal Christian youth. As
he wrote *Hereward*, he was also preparing sermons on David
especially for the undergraduates at Cambridge, and in the first of
these, he included a digression on 'muscular Christianity'.[41]
He wished to clarify his position for the young men whose lives

came directly under his influence. Though generally regarded as a 'clever expression' for a 'new ideal' of the Christian character, it explained nothing to him, he said, but he guessed at two meanings: the first, he hoped, meant 'a healthy manful Christianity', and if this were indeed the meaning, it was acceptable enough, though unnecessary and possibly irreverent; the second, imputed by the *Guardian* (7 May, 1851) fifteen years before, when he had strongly refuted it, was this: 'provided a young man is sufficiently brave, frank, and gallant, he is more or less absolved from the common duties of morality and self-restraint'. If 'muscular Christianity' meant this, then the phrase was anathema to him, for it was 'utterly immoral'. While the four sermons projected the shepherd-king as a model hero, *Hereward the Wake* was meant to dispel at the popular level the last shred of doubt concerning the only 'muscular' Christian of whom Kingsley could approve.

Outlining the history of monasticism, he argued that the monks of the Middle Ages had defied God and human nature in their attempt to unsex themselves and that, as a consequence, they had grown effeminate. Fortunately, that tendency had been offset by 'a new and very fair ideal of manhood', that of knightly perfection. The true knight was loyal to his God and king, bound to defend the right and help the weak. In practice, knighthood was the noblest kind of social Christianity, and the nineteenth-century equivalent was the active Christian gentleman. In danger of losing the knightly ideal, Kingsley's age was pivotal. On the one hand it inculcated a reversion to the sexless Christianity of the Middle Ages and, on the other, it fell back into the heroics of 'our heathen forefathers', who had come, 'slaying, plundering, burning, tossing babes on spear-points' – an age of which Hereward was the last.

David is often Kingsley's model for Hereward, but as we have seen, his hero and his model come to a parting of ways. David has great gifts of personal beauty, daring, prowess, and skill in war. Blest with the chivalry of a medieval knight, he is generous and noble. He is born to lead, to discipline, and to rule. But David also has what Kingsley calls 'a feminine vein'. He is passionately tender. He has a 'vast capacity' for sympathy, which enables him to share the suffering of others. This, indeed, is why the feelings expressed in his Psalms speak age after age to the deepest feelings in man.

As he is dubbed knight, Hereward, too, seems to have all of these qualities. But whereas David slays the lion and the bear 'by God's help', Hereward imagines his strength his own. That Torfrida's gift is more than 'magic armour' is clear from the fact that Hereward never prospers after she leaves him. At his best, he watches while she prays, but of her true value he is only dimly aware. The knowledge of himself as the instrument of a Power not of himself is not given him. He is 'a wild man; his hand [is] against every man, and every man's hand against him', though he dwells 'in the presence of all his brethren'.[42]

As Kingsley's last novel, *Hereward the Wake* is a rude and savage portrait of a rude and savage age. The book is full of fighting and expresses cruelty and bloodthirstiness to the point of nausea. A contemporary critic complained that in *Hereward* Kingsley put 'wild beasts into the skins of Christians', while Kingsley himself called it a 'debauchery' and turned to metaphysics as a restorative. But he was bent on making his point once and for all. The hero may have muscle, indeed, but without the sympathetic love of Christian co-operation and brotherhood that muscle is as the bubble that bursts on the tossing foam. Brute strength, however courageously used, is of the animal nature and belongs to the rough and ready time of youth, whether in individuals or in nations; and with the passing of that youth, which rose against the rude strength of nature – probably most obdurate in the dark fens – passed the great age of the 'muscular' hero.

Hereward is a hero. His spirit broods over the misty fens and the vague and mistier past. It speaks of that wistful and melancholy time when he was the arch representative of his people, our forefathers. In the fine old English legends and ballads that sing of his heroism, strict historical truth may suffer distortion, and popular tradition misrepresent his actions. But the hero whom they commemorate is brave, and courageous, and noble. To err is human, to strive is all. Hereward, with one eye blue and one eye grey, his golden hair in curls upon his neck, lived and loved and, like Everyman, strove in his time with honour, and justice, and right.

Epilogue

Having dissected Kingsley's novels in an attempt to illustrate his purposes in writing them, we have now to see each of them whole, and to regard all of them as an integral part of Kingsley's literary work. As in the beginning we scanned them one by one, so now in order to assess their importance to the English novel as well as Kingsley's place among English novelists, we must look at them in relation to the man himself.

Kingsley has been classed with Disraeli, Mrs. Gaskell, and George Eliot as a writer of political and social novels. Equally, he has much in common with Dickens and Thackeray, and he probably shares more with all of these novelists, with whom he has not been compared, than with Newman and Froude, with whom he has been. Kingsley also wrote historical novels, and again, in this study these have been examined with but little reference to Scott or Lord Lytton, to mention but two authors who wrote in this *genre*. This seeming neglect is in no way intended as a slight to them, nor yet as an indication that Kingsley would have suffered unduly by the comparisons. As Saintsbury succinctly expressed it, 'in inequality Kingsley has few equals, in goodness not many more superiors'. But Kingsley was very much his own man, and little would have been added to our appreciation of him by this approach, though it does help us in placing him.

Kingsley was unique in that, by his own telling, he did not think of himself as a novelist at all. A country parson without the least personal ambition, he was from first to last a busy, hard-working clergyman, who invariably acted hastily on the impulse of the moment to preach out of church as well as in it, and for him as for his generation his novels were all extended but highly imaginative and exciting sermons. Insisting that they were the result of his personal responses to the needs of the moment, he shrank from the literary world and, this being the case, it has seemed right to analyse the novels in terms of the preacher rather than the novelist. And however much we may be inclined to group authors together, the social novelists formed no school and Kingsley, like each of those mentioned, worked independently within the particular sphere of his own experience.

Furthermore, apart from Thomas Hughes with *Tom Brown's School Days*, Kingsley is the only novelist to have deliberately chosen to make himself a popular fictional mouthpiece for one whom he among many regarded as the greatest prophet of the age. The value of Kingsley's novels ultimately lies less in their advocacy of liberality and reform, than in their insistent justification of both on the basis of Christian humanism. Kingsley's inspiration sprang from Maurice whose reading of the Bible had shown his disciple the meaning, both of Christianity and of history, and the novels proclaim that social improvement had necessarily to proceed within the existing framework of society, which for Kingsley meant a Christian dispensation based on Commandments engraven on tablets of stone and interpreted by sacrificial love. A minor prophet proclaiming a major one, Kingsley thus added a new dimension to the novel. In as much as Kingsley's novels represent real life in plots mingling facts with deeply-felt emotion, they are distinctive in expressing the meaning of human destiny, and they may be read for edification and enjoyment in a way that the sermons, I think, cannot. But they reveal Kingsley as a solitary pilgrim proclaiming in the wilderness of a material and industrialized society the spiritual message of another, 'the Master'.

Thirdly, Kingsley's interpretative mission is itself indicative of the nature of his genius. Undeniably possessed of an exceedingly vivid imagination and an exceptional gift in the use of language, Kingsley was by nature a poet. And although he valued his artistic propensities but slightly, without them, his novels like his poetry, would have been impossible. But again he was unique in combining his creative gifts with his mission, and without his artistic skill in the application of this combination his teaching would have had a much feebler wing-stroke. It was this unusual fusion that first marked him for Maurice as the most stimulating and evocative of his disciples.

Actually, Kingsley's strongest affinity lay with the poets of the time although, again, the nature of his genius forced him to work independently of them. Maurice had always looked to Coleridge, so that Kingsley was himself steeped in the poet's speculations as well as Maurice's expository comments on them. And according to Coleridge's *Table Talk* (31 July, 1832), the original design of Wordsworth's *Recluse* was to 'reveal the proof of, and necessity for, the whole state of man and society being subject to, and illustrative of, a redemptive process in operation, showing how this idea reconciled all the anomalies, and promised future glory and restoration' for mankind; and this is precisely the purpose underlying Kingsley's novels. Nor is it strange that the historical scope of the novels should have aimed at vindicating Christian history, since the *Ecclesiastical Sonnets* had earlier expatiated on the theme, surveying Christianity from its introduction into Britain to Wordsworth's 'present'. Under Maurice's guidance, Kingsley, like Tennyson, had adapted these themes from Wordsworth and Coleridge to his own use.

These novels also adumbrate the religious climate of the time and provide original but imaginative documentation for two important group-movements of the period. As simplifications of Maurice's thought, the novels are direct transcriptions of Broad Church principles, while at the same time they not only initiated the Christian Social Movement, but they also provide one of the most interesting primary sources of material on it, and thus they find their niche in English literary and social history.

Finally, these novels have definite significance for us today. A prominent archeologist and historian writing in *The Washington Post* for *The Manchester Guardian Weekly* (25 January, 1976) on 'The Aging of America', Mr. Theodore Wertime feels that after two hundred years of history the United States is 'showing the same symptoms as Rome in the second century A.D.' According to him, the malaise that destroyed Rome is now rearing 'its ugly vexing head' in his country, so that his countrymen must return, he says, to the traditional human values. 'To lose the mandate of heaven,' he declares, 'is to lose the loyalties of one's citizens who, are now beginning to 'beat a rapid retreat back to personal modules of survival: the family, farm, manor, commune, church . . .'.

The church? Today there are large numbers of people who feel that the church is moribund, that it might better be absorbed into a department of government where the clergy, slickly ensconced behind chrome and plate-glass, could care for the unemployed, the poor, the old and, increasingly, the middle-aged, with efficiency and dispatch. But it is seriously to be doubted whether a 'church' of this kind would enjoy 'the mandate of heaven'.

Here Kingsley's novels can help us. In a civilization determinedly materialistic and increasingly mundane and selfish, they still remind us as they reminded Kingsley's generation, that Christianity was divinely founded to humanize and redeem mankind. In upholding the cumulative wisdom of the ages, they show our present as they showed Kingsley's, that in the onward rush of time into eternity, our generation, like every other, can only resolve its dilemma by working *sub specie aeternitatis* in partnership with a Providence vitally alive in the conscience of each man, whose Godward tendency is but the natural result of that conscience socially orientated. These novels offer a corrective for unworthy tendencies in our day as they did in Kingsley's, and they challenge us to face the calamity of a society grown confused and cynical, and apathetic to all but acquisitiveness because it has cut the roots of its spiritual heritage.

Notes

CHAPTER 1

1 G.M. Young, *Victorian Essays*, chosen and introduced by W.D. Handcock (OUP, 1962), p. 150.
2 Unless otherwise indicated, all quotations of Kingsley are taken from *The Works of Charles Kingsley* (28 vols., Macmillan, 1880–5), hereafter abbreviated to *Works*, and the reference noted by volume, Chapter, and page.
3 *Works*, II, 1, 8–11.
4 *Ibid.*, III, 11, 22.
5 *Ibid.*, IV, XXII, 280 ff.
6 *Ibid.*, IV, XI, 128.
7 *Ibid.*, VIII, VXII, 299.
8 *Ibid.*, XI, Prelude, 11 ff.
9 *Ibid.*, XX, Appendix, 302.
10 The biographical material is taken from *Charles Kingsley: His Letters and Memories of His Life*, edited by his wife, 5th edition (2 volumes, Henry S. King, 1877): hereafter, *LM*.
11 *The Kingdom of Christ or Hints to a Quaker respecting the Principles, Constitution and Ordinances of the Catholic Church* (1838). A new edition, based on the Second edition of 1842, edited by Alec R. Vidler (2 volumes, 1958), has been used here.
12 In a letter to Lady Welling. See *Echoes of a Larger Life*, edited by Mrs. Henry Cust (1929), p. 68.
13 *LM*, I, 101.
14 *Ibid.*, 127.
15 'Recollections of Rev. Charles Kingsley', *The Cheshire Observer* (6 February, 1875).
16 *LM*, I, 308.
17 Of the eight *Tracts on Christian Socialism*, four were by Maurice, three by J.M.F. Ludlow, and one by Thomas Hughes.
18 *LM*, I, 84.
19 *Ibid.*, 397.
20 *The Kingdom of Christ*, I, 125 f., 133, 153.
21 Maurice was a disciple of Samuel Taylor Coleridge. See his Dedication in *The Kingdom of Christ*, II, 348–64.
22 Maurice, *Subscription No Bondage* (1835), pp. 46–7.
23 Herbert Butterfield, *Christianity and History* (Fontana, 1958), p. 43.
24 'Moral and Metaphysical Philosophy', *Encyclopaedia Metropolitana* (1839), pp. 557, 673; hereafter *MM*; Maurice, *The Friendship of Books* (1874), p. 141.

25 E.D.W., 'Letters on the Bible No. IV', *The Educational Magazine*, edited by F.D. Maurice, II (New Series, 1840), 100 ff.

26 *MM*, pp. 561–5.

27 Maurice, *Lectures on Ecclesiastical History* (1854), pp. 138–362 *passim*; Maurice, *The Friendship of Books*, pp. 136–7.

28 *MM*, p. 599.

29 *LM*, I, 338.

30 *Works*, XX, 81; V, 139.

31 Maurice, *Learning and Working*, edited with an introduction by W.E. Styler (1968), p. 78.

32 *Works*, XX, VIII, 254.

33 *Works*, III, XXII, 231; *The Friendship of Books*, p. 53; Maurice, *Social Mortality*, p. 150.

34 Paraphrased from S.T. Coleridge, *Lay Sermons* (1852), Appendix B, p. 77; A.L. (copied), f. 147, Br. Mus. Add. MS. 3632.

35 S.T. Coleridge, *Literary Remains*, II, 372; 'Language in the Bible', *The Times Literary Supplement* (24 March, 1961), p. 184.

36 *LM*, I, 21.

37 *Ibid.*, 22.

38 *Ibid.*, II, 242.

39 *Ibid.*, I, 300; *The Times* (30 May, 1970); *Friendship of Books*, p. 150; Alice D. Snyder, *Coleridge on Logic and Learning* (1929), p. 138.

40 *LM*, I, 302.

41 Leon Edel, *Literary Biography* (1957), pp. 3, 231.

42 *Varieties of Religious Experience* (1952), p. 186.

43 James Strachan, 'Conversion', *Encyclopaedia of Religion and Ethics* (1911), IV, 104.

44 *Works* II, III, 37.

45 J.A.R. Marriott, *Charles Kingsley, Novelist* (1892), p. 27, for this and the directive quotation above.

46 *Works*, XI, 251.

47 *Ibid.*, III, VIII, 93.

48 *Ibid.*, VI, XXVIII, 504.

49 *LM*, II, 281.

CHAPTER 2

1 Marriott, p. 17, but affirmed by all writers on the period from Cazamian to P.J. Keating.

2 *Works*, XXI, XI, 85.

3 *The Christian Socialist* (2 November, 1850), I, 3.

4 Charles E. Raven, *Christian Socialism 1848–1854* (1920, reprinted 1968), p. 106.

5 R.G. Gammage, *The History of the Chartist Movement 1837–1857* (1894, reprinted 1968), pp. 310 ff.

6 *Works*, XV, 249.

7 *LM*, I, 299.

8 *Ibid.*, I, 305.

9 *Works*, I, 259.
10 *LM*, I, 306.
11 Raven, p. 108.
12 *The Life of Frederick Denison Maurice*, edited by his son, Frederick Maurice (2 volumes, 1884), I, 463.
13 Published monthly under his immediate inspection, and edited by F.R. Trehonnais (July, 1849), p. 5.
14 'On the Development of the Principle of Socialism in France', *Politics*, pp. 24, 41, 89.
15 *Life of F.D. Maurice*, II, 497.
16 For the Letter, see p. 58 of *Politics; Life of F.D. Maurice*, I, 476.
17 *LM*, I, 330.
18 A.L.S. (1852): Cambridge University Library Add. MS. 7348, Bundle 17.
19 Lucien Wolf, *The Life of the First Marquess of Ripon* (1921), pp. 21–42; A.L. (copied) f. 11 (25 May, 1852): Br. Mus. MS. Add 43621; Wolf, 36 n.
20 *Life of F.D. Maurice*, II, 128–32; Cp. 557–9.
21 *The Quarterly Review*, LXXXIX (1851), 491–543; *Life of F.D. Maurice*, II, 71–4.
22 'Article on Christian Socialism', XCIII (1851), 1–33.
23 *LM*, I, 288–9.
24 *Works*, XV, vi, 296.
25 *LM*, I, 315.

CHAPTER 3

1 *Works*, II, xiv, 229.
2 In a letter to Benjamin Bailey, dated 23 January, 1818.
3 Volume XXXVIII (July, 1848), 102.
4 Acts 9: 1–20.
5 A.J. Hartley, 'Christian Socialism and Conversion', *Theology*, LXX (December, 1967), 542–9.
6 R.H. Murray, *Group Movements Through the Ages* (1935), p. 300.
7 Maurice's first *Tract on Christian Socialism*.
8 See Maurice's *Theological Essays*, edited from the second edition of 1853, with an introduction by Canon Edward Carpenter, (1957). The concluding essay – 'On Eternal Life and Eternal Death', is especially interesting.
9 A.L.S., F.E.K. to her sister, Mrs. (John Ashley) Warre (23 January, 1850): AM. MSS. 14575, R.H. Taylor Folder, The Parrish Collection, Princeton University Library.
10 *LM*, I, 44.
11 *Works*, I, 267.
12 *Ibid.*
13 *Life of F.D. Maurice* (1884), II, 58.
14 A.L.S., J.M.F.L. to C.K. and Mrs. C.K. (15 July, 1848): Add. MS. 7348, Bundle 16, Fitzwilliam Library, Cambridge University.
15 *LM*, I, 305.

CHAPTER 4

1 R.G. Gammage, *The History of the Chartist Movement 1837–1854* (Merlin Reprint, 1969), p. 30.
2 *Life of F.D. Maurice*, I, 519.
3 *The North British Review* (1852), reprinted as 'Burns and His School', *Literary and General Essays, Works*, XX, p. 127.
4 *LM*, I, 184.
5 'A Visit to the Cholera Districts of Bermondsey', p. 4.
6 *The Unknown Mayhew* Selections from the *Morning Chronicle* 1849–1850, edited by E.P. Thompson and Eileen Yeo (Merlin Reprint, 1971), pp. 196–227; Cp. *Works*, III, xxxv.
7 Note 5, above, Cp. *Works*, III, xxxv, 370.
8 *Works*, III, xiv.
9 *Life and Labour*, reprinted from *Nineteenth Century* and edited by Charles Booth (1889), I, 209.
10 A.L.S. (6 March, 1850), C.K. to Chapman and Hall, University of Illinois.
11 *LM*, I, 247.
12 R.H. Tawney, *Religion and the Rise of Capitalism* (Murray, 1926), p. 213.
13 *LM*, I, 127.
14 Br. Mus. Add. MS. 41297.
15 William James, *Varieties of Religious Experience* (1952), p. 186.
16 Leslie Stephen, 'Charles Kingsley', *Cornhill Magazine*, XXXV (January–June, 1877), 436.
17 *The Life of Thomas Cooper* by himself (1872), p. 290; Cp. Louis Cazamian, *Kingsley et Thomas Cooper* (Thèse, Paris, 1903); Robert J. Conklin, *Thomas Cooper the Chartist 1805–1892* (1935).
18 *LM*, I, 120.
19 M. Kaufmann, 'The Theory of Christian Socialism', *The British Quarterly*, LXXX (1884), 316–38, particularly pp. 326, 336.
20 A.L.S. (6 March, 1850), C.K. to Chapman and Hall, University of Illinois.
21 *LM*, I, 269.
22 *Ibid.*, 197.
23 Thomas Carlyle, *Chartism* (1840), pp. 46–8; Cp. H.J.C. Grierson, *Carlyle and Hitler* (1933), pp. 26–7.
24 Br. Mus. Add. MS. 41297, f. 99–101: A.L.S. C.K. to M. (23 November, 1856).
25 *Life of F.D. Maurice*, II, 54.
26 *LM*, I, 245.
27 For Carlyle's view of Maurice, see J.A. Froude, *Thomas Carlyle* (1884), I, 126.
28 *LM*, I, 242.

CHAPTER 5

1 S.T. Coleridge, *Biographia Literaria*, ed. by Shawcross, I, 109–10, and Shawcross's note, p. 250. Understanding is sensuous, experiential and, in

animals, instinctual. 'Reason implies all that distinguishes man from the animals'. It includes animal understanding plus self-consciousness, but it is essentially supersensuous and sciential, instinct with powers of reflection, comparison, and suspension of judgment.

2 G.M. Trevelyan, 'History and Fiction', *The Cornhill Magazine*, New Series LII (January to June, 1922), 527–39; Cp. *LM*, I, 263.

3 Socrates Scholasticus, *History*, *A.D. 324 to 340*, being volume IV of *The Greek Ecclesiastical Historians* (1844). See Book VII, Ch. xv.

4 *The Letters of Synesius of Cyrene*, translated into English with Introduction and Notes by Augustine Fitzgerald (OUP, 1926).

5 *Life of F.D.M.*, II, 56.

6 *LM*, I, 268.

7 Gibbon, VI, 12: 'The *Parbolani* of Alexandria were a charitable corporation instituted during the plague of Gallienus, to visit the sick and to bury the dead. They gradually enlarged, abused, and sold the privileges of their order. Their outrageous conduct during the reign of Cyril provoked the emperor to deprive the patriarch of their nomination, and to restrain their number to five or six hundred. But these restraints were transient and ineffectual'. Gibbon VI, 12, who cites Theodosian as his source.

8 *Works*, IV, v, 62.

9 Augustine, *The City of God* (Everyman, 2 vols.), I, xii–xv; II, xiv; *LM*, I, 335: '. . . but beloved Augustine, with all his calm grace and large-heartedness, and polished subtlety and learning, *he* is the redeeming point on the south of the Mediterranean'.

10 Ch. xv of Book VII of Socrates' account is just over a page in length. The shells appear to have been pieces of tile.

11 *Works*, IV, xiii, 148.

12 *Ibid.*, IV, vi, 75.

13 See note 1, above.

14 Maurice appears to have directed Kingsley's story instalment by instalment. See *Life of F.D.M.*, II, 56–7; 108–11; 140–3; 166–7.

15 For the misuse of mythology and the difference between Platonic and Neoplatonic uses, see *MM*, 634–5.

16 *Life of F.D.M.*, II, 140–3.

17 *Works*, IV, xvii, 199.

18 Maurice's *Epistle to the Hebrews*, pp. lxxix, cxxvi, reveal Maurice's views as Raphael's.

19 *Works*, IV, xviii, 203.

20 *Life of F.D.M.*, II, 109; 140–3; *MM*, 638: Maurice credits Augustine with Christianizing 'the Socratic doctrine of a living spirit in man' against which his nature is in constant conflict in the gradual subjugation of his animal nature. Augustine thus posits the doctrine of a good and evil principle by which national no less than individual history proceeds.

21 *Works*, IV, xxi, 267.

22 *Ibid.*, 273.

23 *MM*, 637. Maurice is distinguishing between the primary and the secondary imagination. See *Biographia Literaria*, I, 202.

24 *Works*, XVII, iii, 93; *LM*, I, 336.

25 *Ibid.*, IV, xv, 175.
26 *Ibid.*, IV, I, 9.
27 Br. Mus. Add. MS. 3668, A.L.S., f. 62: C.K. to T.H., [?1852].
28 Rosemond Tuve, *Allegorical Imagery* (Princeton, 1966), pp. 57–8.
29 *LM*, I, 354.
30 R.B. Martin, *The Dust of Combat*, p. 143.
31 *De Civitate Dei* (Everyman, 1950), II, xix, 17, 255.
32 *Life of F.D.M.*, II, 140–3.
33 Edited with an Introduction by Edward F. Carpenter, 1957.
34 *Life of F.D.M.*, II, 108–11. In this letter of 11 February, 1852, Maurice declares that this passage 'taught [him] more than all the metaphysical books [he] ever came in contact with, and threw back a wonderful light on Plato'. He refers to the same passage in another letter of 27 June, 1853: see *Life of F.D.M.*, II, 166–7.

CHAPTER 6

1   Volumes III and IV were published in 1856. Kingsley reviewed them in the *North British Review*, LI (November, 1856). See his *Works*, XVI, 209.
2   *Works*, V, 58.
3   *Ibid.*, VI, xxxi, 557.
4   R.G. Collingwood, *The Historical Imagination*, An Inaugural Lecture delivered before the University of Oxford on 28 October, 1935 (OCP 1935).
5   Maurice, *The Friendship of Books*, p. 136.
6   C.A. Patrides, *The Grand Design of God* (1972), p. 38.
7   John W. Dodds, *The Age of Paradox* (1953), pp. 30, 439, 441.
8   Elizabeth Longford, *Victoria R.I.* (1970), p. 301.
9   *Works*, XVII, 3–103.
10 *LM*, I, 433.
11 Cecil Woodham-Smith, *Florence Nightingale 1820–1910* (Penguin, 1955), p. 190.
12 Although Lord Cardigan with unquestioning bravery actually led the Brigade, the order which resulted in the charge is signed [Captain] R. Airey, who says, 'Lord Raglan wishes the cavalry to advance rapidly to the front, follow the enemy and try to prevent the enemy carrying away the guns. Troop horse Artillery may accompany. French cavalry is on your left. Immediate.' Captain Lewis Edward Nolan delivered the note. The account is movingly told by Cecil Woodham-Smith, *The Reason Why* (McGraw-Hill, 1954), pp. 167, 228–38.
13 *LM*, I, 434.
14 A.S. Collins's introduction to Kingsley's *Westward Ho!* (Univ. Tutorial Press, 1938), p. 7.
15 *Hakluyt's Voyages*, introduction by John Masefield (8 vols., 1907, reprinted 1926), II, 369.
16 A.L.S., C.K. to Thomas Longstaff (7 September, 1855): Pierpont Morgan Library.

17 *Ibid.*
18 Reported to the writer by Miss Marjorie Ackland, Bideford, North Devon.
19 Shakespeare's play, Act III, Sc. I.
20 *Works*, XXI, XXVII, 371.
21 A.D. Innes, p. x.
22 Reprinted from *The Devonian Year Book* (1912).
23 A.L.S., C.K. to Sir——, (26 November, 1855): Pierpont Morgan Library.
24 *LM*, I, 446.
25 R.C. Collingwood, *The Historical Imagination*, pp. 14–15.
26 For new light on the Newman–Kingsley controversy, see G. Egner, *Apologia Pro Charles Kingsley* (Sheed & Ward, 1969).
27 James Williamson, *The Age of Drake* (Adam and Charles Black, 1965); Kenneth R. Andrews, *Drakes Voyages* (Weidenfeld & Nicholson, 1967); J.E. Neale, *Queen Elizabeth* (Penguin, 1952); Neville Williams, *Elizabeth I Queen of England* (Sphere, 1967).
28 *Encyclopaedia of Religion and Ethics*, VII (1914), 500–5.
29 Vol. I, 119.
30 *Virgil's Works*, translated by J. W. Mackail with an introduction by Charles L. Durham (Modern Library, 1934) Bk. I, line 364.
31 The mainland of South America from Peru and along the Caribbean Sea, particularly from Panama to the Orinoco.
32 Christopher Lloyd, *The British Seaman 1200–1860*. A social survey (London: Paladin, 1970), p. 32.
33 *LM*, I, 433.
34 Kingsley incorporated the last words of Sir Richard Grenville in his novel, p. 124; 'Here die I, Richard Grenville, with a joyful and quiet mind; for that I have ended my life as a true soldier ought, fighting for his country, queen, religion, and honour: my soul willingly departing from this body, leaving behind the lasting fame of having behaved as every valiant soldier is in his duty bound to do'.
35 Drake's 'noble prayer' uttered in the spring of 1588: see Colonel E.T. Clifford, 'Drake's Treasure' (24 July 1912), in *Transactions of the Devonshire Association*, XLIV, 514: 'That the Lord of all strength will put into Her Majesty and her people courage and boldness; not to fear any invasion of her own country, but to seek God's enemies and Her Majesty's where they may be found'.
36 *Works*, VI, XXXIII, 584.
37 *Ibid.*, 585.
38 Maurice Evans, *Spenser's Anatomy of Heroism* (CUP, 1970), p. 19.
39 John Erskine Hankins, *Source and Meaning in Spenser's Allegory*, A Study of *The Faerie Queene* (OCP, 1971), p. 48.
40 John F. Danby, *Poets on Fortune's Hill* (Faber, 1952), p. 51.
41 F.D. Maurice, *Moral and Metaphysical Philosophy* (2 vols., 1872), I, 226.
42 J.A.K. Thomson, *The Ethics of Aristotle*, The Nicomachean Ethics Translated (Allen & Unwin, 1953), p. 218.
43 *F.Q.*, IV, IX, I.
44 *Works*, VI, XIX, 344.
45 *F.Q.*, IV, VI, 43.

46 Hankins, pp. 2, 54, 141–3, 150.
47 *Works*, VI, IX, 182.
48 DNB: For Brooke, II (to 1900), p. 1336; for Selwyn, XVII (to 1900) p. 1170.

CHAPTER 7

1 *Works*, VIII, XIX, 353. For variant readings, see *Works*, I, 216; *LM*, I, 487,
2 *Sanitary and Social Essays, Works*, XXII, XV, 157.
3 S.T. Coleridge, *Lay Sermons* (3rd ed., 1853), pp. 19, 70–3; Maurice, *The Conscience* (1868); *The Kingdom of Christ*, II, 43; *Works*, XIX, 201; *Life of F.D.M.*, I, 371.
4 Maurice, *Patriarchs and Lawgivers of the Old Testament*, 2nd ed. (1855). pp. 266–8.
5 *Works*, VI, XXI, 377.
6 *LM*, II, 44.
7 Philip Magnus, *Gladstone* (reprinted 1970), p. 115; *The Observer of the Nineteenth Century*, selected by Marion Miliband, introduction by Asa Briggs (1966), p. 175.
8 J.A.R. Marriott, *England since Waterloo* (1927), pp. 234–51.
9 Norman Longmate, *King Cholera The Biography of a Disease* (1966), p. 191.
10 General Board of Health, *Appendix to Report of The Committee for Scientific Inquiries in Relation to the Cholera Epidemic of 1854* (1855).
11 Charles Creighton, *A History of Epidemics in Britain*, 2 vols. (1894), II, 851 n.
12 J.B. Atlay, *Sir Henry Wentworth Acland, Bart., Regius Professor of Medicine in the University of Oxford A Memoir* (1903), pp. 183, 186.
13 Henry Wentworth Acland, *Memoir of the Cholera at Oxford in the Year 1854, With Considerations Suggested by the Epidemic* (1856), p. 6.
14 Lawrence Wright, *Clean and Decent The Fascinating History of the Bathroom and WC* (1960), pp. 75, 108, 144, 148, 156; *King Cholera*, pp. 144, 176, 194; see also Cecil Woodham-Smith, *Florence Nightingale 1820–1910* (1950).
15 Guy Kendall, *Charles Kingsley and His Ideas* (1947), p. 114.
16 Br. Mus. Add. MS. 41299, A.L. (copied), f. 200, 7 December, 1875: Rev. Derwent Coleridge to Mrs. Charles Kingsley.
17 *LM*, II, 23.
18 Edited by Viscount Ingestre, *Meliora : or, Better Times to Come* (2nd series, 1853), p. 7.
19 *King Cholera*, p. 171.
20 *LM*, I, 413.
21 *Ibid.*, 439.
22 George Brimley, 'Kingsley's *Two Years Ago*', *The Spectator* (14 February, 1857), 176–7; '*Two Years Ago* by Charles Kingsley', *British Quarterly Review* (January–April, 1857), 399–420; '*Two Years Ago*', *The Eclectic Review*, I (Jan.–June, 1857), 499–515; '*Two Years Ago*', *The Saturday Review* (21 February, 1857), 176–7; '*Two Years Ago*', *The Athenaeum* (14 February, 1857), 212.

23   *King Cholera*, p. 171.
24   *Works*, XVIII, ix, 231.
25   *LM*, II, 19.
26   Margaret Farrand Thorp, *Charles Kingsley 1819–1875* (1937), p. 128.
27   *King Cholera*, p. 194.
28   E.C. Rickards, *Felicia Skene of Oxford: A Memoir* (1902), pp. 97–111.
29   S.T. Coleridge, *Biographia Literaria*, ed. Shawcross (1965), I, 62.
30   *LM*, II, 43.
31   *Ibid*.
32   Bernard Martin, *The Dust of Combat* (1959), p. 203.
33   *Works*, XXII, xv, 157.

CHAPTER 8

1   Edited by Norman MacLeod, one of Queen Victoria's chaplains for Scotland. See p. 5.
2   Edward Trollope, 'Hereward the Saxon Patriot', *Associated Architectural Societies Reports and Papers* (1861), VI, part 1, p. 18; Psalm 127: 12.
3   J.W. Day, *A History of the Fens* (1954), p. 43; H.C. Darby, *The Mediaeval Fenland* (1940).
4   *Works*, XII, 301.
5   *Works*, XV.
6   *Ibid.*, XI.
7   *Ibid.*, 263.
8   *LM*, I, 182.
9   *Ibid.*, 151.
10   For the best modern version, see *The History of the Norman Conquest of England* (6 volumes, 1867–79), IV, 454–87.
11   Drawn from *A Short History of the Norman Conquest in 1888*. See pp. 151–2.
12   T.F. Tout, DNB.
13   Volume I, 224–39.
14   *The Anglo-Norman Metrical Chronicle*, edited by Wright (1850).
15   Appendix 3, *Anglo-Norman Metrical Chronicle*, edited by Wright (1850).
16   Thomas Wright, *Essays on the Literature, etc., of England during the Middle Ages* (2 vols., 1846).
17   Thomas Wright, 'On the Poetry of History', *Essays* (1846), pp. 82–90.
18   Charles Kingsley, *The Heroes*, introduction by John Warrington (Dent paperback, 1970) includes 'The Twelve Labours of Hercules' by Grace Rhys. See also, Joseph Campbell, *The Hero with a Thousand Faces* (1961).
19   *Works*, XI, xx, 259.
20   *Ibid.*, XII, 165.
21   *Ibid*, xx, 255.
22   *Ibid.*, 256.
23   *Ibid.*, xv, 262.
24   *Ibid.*, 193.
25   *Ibid.*, XXVI, 315.

26 *The Anglo-Saxon Chronicle*, edited with a translation by Benjamin Thorpe (1861), II, 177.

27 *Works*, XI, XXVII, 339.

28 Shakespeare, *Antony and Cleopatra*, III, IV, 22.

29 *Works*, XI, XXXVIII, 466.

30 *Ibid.*, XXXI, 377.

31 *Ibid.*, XLI, 496.

32 *Ibid.*, XV, 190.

33 *Ibid.*, XXV, 311 n.

34 *Ibid.*, XXXII, 389.

35 *Ibid.*, XXVII, 341.

36 *Ibid.*, XXXII, 385.

37 *Ibid.*, XXIII, 285.

38 *Ibid.*, XXXII, 391 n.

39 *Ibid.*, XXXIII, 404.

40 *Harold The Last of the Saxon Kings* (Knebworth edition), p. 409 n. The novel was first published in 1848.

41 *Works*, XXV, David, Sermon 1.

42 Genesis: XVI: 12.

Index